The
The Woman &
The Wonderful Saviour

Dear Ayo,

We really appreciate your friendship and kind heart.

Praying for you to find more light in the knowledge of God's unconditional love for you.

Best wishes from Sign, Debby and Kids.

SIGNS AND WONDERS

: 9-10-23

Edited by: Debby Yinka Wonders
Book Cover Art: Maintained Lot Productions
Book Layout and Interior Design: Wonderside Media

CONTENTS

INTRODUCTION

The Well, Woman and Wonderful Saviour is a book that largely centres on the book of John chapter four (4). It has been divided into three (3) parts for easy reading and understanding.

Part One: The Well is a typology to reveal man's spiritual thirst for a personal relationship with God, which if not achieved, leaves him doomed even in the face of the most refreshing wells of water. Although the well addresses man's physical need for water, it exposes his dependence on nature rather than his dominion over it.

Part Two: The Woman at the well is a metaphor to represent the disposition of every sinner before they meet Jesus and the difference that encounter makes in their lives.

Part Three: The Wonderful Saviour reveals God's goodness to mankind in sending rain. Even so, though the water helps him stay alive physically, mankind remains doomed with spiritual death because of sin, unless he ultimately receives the gift of the Son of God as his Saviour.

John 4: 1-4

1. When therefore the Lord knew how the Pharisees had heard that Jesus made and baptized more disciples than John,

2. although in fact it was not Jesus who baptized, but his disciples.

3. He left Judaea, and departed again into Galilee.

4. And he must needs go through Samaria.

In this story, God's grand plan comes into play as the Jew's rejection of Jesus as the messiah opens the door of salvation to Samaria and other gentile nations. Jesus left Judea for Samaria, having known the Jews to be bitter towards the success of his ministry. This aggression and hostility was because they didn't believe he was the messiah. Having been rejected, Jesus turned to the Samaritans. On getting to Samaria he stops at Sychar, which means 'drunken', where he meets a woman with a history of failed marriages. And isn't it striking that this woman, coming from 'drunkenness' (which in a sense implies a kind of satisfaction or a state of saturation) comes out with an empty pot, searching for water to quench her thirst? At the end of the 'illusive joy' that sin provides, it only leaves its victim lonely, searching for true satisfaction. Though the water pot could occasionally provide this woman with water to quench her physical thirst, her problem required more than an occasional sip of water. Emotionally, a series of failed marriages had left her drained. Spiritually, she was lost, with no hope of ever reaching God (whose dealings at that time was limited to the Jews), especially as she was a Samaritan.

In this book, we will uncover how sin brought about the emptiness our world currently suffers from. And as we will discover, the true cure for this emptiness is spiritual. Only a deep, intimate and personal relationship with a loving Jesus can make the difference. What an amazing story this is, that reassures us of a love that's indescribable. What an assurance that we have a saviour who knows us more than anyone, yet won't condemn us. We may not know how to reach him but he sure knows where to meet us and he is never far away. He is patiently waiting for us to encounter his love, so that we can find true satisfaction for our thirst. Sin will certainly leave its victim drained, but praise God, there is a Wonderful Saviour who has come to make us overflow with Living water.

As you read this book, I pray that you encounter the same Jesus who brought transformation, peace, joy and satisfaction to the woman of Samaria.

PART ONE:
THE WELL

THE WELL

E arth is called a blue planet because from outer space it appears blue. The reason for this phenomenon is due to the Earth being covered by water. All living things on Earth need water. Scientifically, Man is about 60 percent water. Plants are up to or over 90 percent water.

In photographs taken from space, we can see that our planet has more water than land. It is unexpected and somewhat inconceivable that less than three percent of Earth's water is freshwater. According to the U.S. Geological Survey, most of that three percent is inaccessible. Over 68 percent of the freshwater on Earth is found in icecaps and glaciers, and just over 30 percent is found in groundwater. Only about 0.3 percent of our freshwater is found in the surface water of lakes, rivers, and swamps. Of all the water on Earth, more than 99 percent of Earth's water is unusable by humans and many other living things! In photographs taken from space, we can see that our planet has more water than land. It is unexpected and somewhat inconceivable that less than three percent of Earth's water is freshwater.

According to the U.S. Geological Survey, most of that three percent is inaccessible. Over 68 percent of the freshwater on Earth is found in icecaps and glaciers, and just over 30 percent is found in groundwater. Only about 0.3 percent of our freshwater is found in the surface water of lakes, rivers, and swamps. Of all the water on Earth, more than 99 percent of Earth's water is unusable by humans and many other living things. (https://education.nationalgeographic.org/resource/earths-fresh-water/). To survive, humans have had to find a way to store this all-important colourless, odourless and transparent liquid. The invention of wells was one of the several such attempts to make water more readily available for human use. Although water seems to be everywhere around man, its purest form isn't. The invention of wells made water to be available at least in a form that is almost completely free from impurities.

At the time of this story, Jews used water for their survival and that of their animals. They also used water for ceremonial purification and cleansing. People would collect water from natural sources such as free-running streams, fountains, and springs or from artificial sources such as wells, water systems, reservoirs, and cisterns.

1
BIBLE ACCOUNT OF WELLS

W̶e don't have much description of the physical outlook of wells from the Bible, however, there are some clues here and there. For instance, we know that the wells had to be dug (Gen. 26:18-22), covers were made for them (Gen. 29:1-3), a bucket-like object (fetching can) was used to draw water (Gen. 24:20) from it.

The task of fetching water from the wells was mostly a feminine one according to Bible history. The Bible records that young unmarried women went out in the evening to fetch water (Gen. 24:11) and they used pitchers, pots, jars, jugs (Gen. 24:16) or animal skin bottles (Gen. 21:19), to take the water home.

Due to how essential water was for survival, wars often broke out between communities over the ownership and possession of wells. Those who couldn't fight or own a well by any other means had no choice but to live at the mercy of those who could. The Bible notes that when Abraham died, there was striving between the herdsmen of Gerar and Isaac's, with each claiming; "The water is ours" (Gen. 26:18-20). The men of Gerar resorted to a fight so they could lay claim on a well that wasn't theirs.

Wells were also notable as the place to find a good spouse. Whenever ladies went out to fetch water, young unmarried men would make their way to the well. The reason was that in those days, wells were the only place young men could meet beautiful damsels without the prying eyes of their fathers and other male relatives. Rebekah, Rachel and Zipporah all met their suitors or prospective husbands at the well (Gen. 24:10-22, 29:10, Exod. 2:15-21). It is somehow difficult to relate with this story in the 21st century because we don't need wells to be dug, fought over, bought or inherited to survive in many parts of the world. Modern technology has made it easier and possible to have water in a purer form than what wells could provide back then. And young men certainly do not need any wells to find love, not when we now have social media. Why go to a well when you can go to her Facebook Wall, right?

Wells Are Limited But Man's Needs Are Unlimited

Depending on the capacity of the well available, in sparsely populated areas, water supplies could sustain the people for longer periods of time. Still, with time, humans will exhaust even the largest wells. It therefore appears that man himself is a well that no well made by humans can fully satisfy. The well is man's way to meet his needs. It is his effort to beat lack. A well doesn't create water, it can only hold whatever it gets. If there's no external source to feed it water, the well will dry up.

Man's inventions never bring him complete satisfaction or perfectly meet his needs. And as someone rightly observed, when an engineer solves one problem he creates another. If we ever make a well that can hold a large enough amount of water, we will have created another problem in the process.

Using a community well like the one in this story would usually present its own challenges. You will have to be strong enough to pull up the pail of water out of the well, else you were at the mercy of others. You were also likely to face long queues, with all ladies going out to fetch water at certain times. The desperation to get water could result in fights. Inadvertently, the well's limited capacity would become a challenge as the human population grew and seasons changed. During the rainy season, the well would hold more water, but scarcity was an issue in the dry season.

Since the sun is usually hottest around noon, it makes sense that everyone hurries to fetch water from the well in the cool of the day, for convenience and ease. Understandably, this became the logical thing or the 'normal way', much like an unwritten rule in the community for fetching water. Individuals usually complied with this and parents raised their children to conform to the standard. Choosing to go to the well outside the 'normal time' was often interpreted as laziness. Such a person was an outlier, irresponsible and without good home training.

Genesis 24:11

> *And he made his camels to kneel down without the city by a well of water at the time of the evening, even the time that women go out to draw water.*

As we end this chapter, let's consider some important questions: With the creation of the well, has man been able to end his desperate craving for water? Can man create or influence rain to ensure a steady supply at the well? And even if mankind had all the water it needs, will that translate into complete rest and satisfaction? In creating the well, man has fully established that he has a need. However, water is not the only need of man, and if he eventually meets all his water needs, he still has other needs that must be met. Man's inability to control the seasons and ensure constant water availability, and his inability to meet other needs, shows that man requires something beyond himself to help him.

Why do men study the weather? Why do communities worship demons who claim to be in-charge of water (rain, rivers and seas)? It will also be necessary to ask, where do needs come from? Why does it seem like all through man's life, he simply jumps from meeting one need to another. Why are man's needs endless?

PART TWO:
THE WOMAN

THE WOMAN

On his way from Judea to Galilee, Jesus had to pass through Samaria. It was there in Samaria, that the woman met him, by the well. She had come to fetch water at a time of the day unusual for women to do that chore. Without doubt, this Samaritan woman was one of those women to be considered lazy, an outlaw, irresponsible and without proper upbringing, because she went to the well at a time women don't normally go out for water. At the time she went, no one ought to be there, so she must have been avoiding people. It should have been easier to go to the well in the company of other ladies than alone, but this woman could not dare. In addition to her record of multiple failed romantic relationships, she was divorced, yet cohabiting with someone who was not her husband. She would definitely come under severe criticism and backlash from her community. How condemned and dirty she must have felt. The shaming and ridicule from the other women must have been her fears. And if she could not stand up to man's judgement, she would have been more scared of standing before

God. She must have concluded 'hell at last' and nothing less for someone like her.

Experience, they say, is the best teacher, but this woman's case proves nothing could be further from the truth. One would think that after five failed marriages, she would have gotten enough wisdom from her experiences to be able to handle the sixth one, yet this time she was even more foolish. She was already living with a man who wasn't her husband. The woman in this story is from Samaria. Someone from Samaria is called a Samaritan. Samaritans are a mixed race; offspring from an intermarriage with the settlers from other nations brought in by the Assyrians to settle among them.

Ancient Samaria and Jerusalem had a lot in common in the ninth and eighth centuries B.C.E. Both were part of David and Solomon's United Kingdom of Israel in the tenth century, and both became capitals when Israel split into the southern kingdom of Judah and the northern kingdom of Israel. Jerusalem became the capital of Judah, and Samaria, Israel (https://www.biblicalarchaeology.org/daily/archaeology-today/biblical-archaeology-topics/ancient-samaria-and-jerusalem/). You may well be aware of the New Testament parable of the good Samaritan, but you probably don't know that there are still around 800 ancient Israelite Samaritans living today (https://www.bbc.com/travel/article/20180828-the-last-of-the-good-samaritans).

2
THE HISTORY OF SAMARIA

During the reign of Rehoboam the son of Solomon, Israel ceased to be united. It became divided into two kingdoms; the southern kingdom led by Rehoboam and the northern kingdom of Israel, led by the rebel Jeroboam (1 Kings 12). The southern kingdom was made up of Judah and the majority of the tribe of Benjamin, with Jerusalem as her capital. The other 10 tribes and part of the tribe of Benjamin who didn't accept Rehoboam as their king, made up the northern kingdom. The region of Samaria was assigned to the house of Joseph, that is, to the tribe of Ephraim and to half of the tribe of Manasseh. Thus, Samaria was part of the northern kingdom. Jeroboam, afraid that the kingdoms might reunite one day due to the religious bond between them, moved to separate the Israelites in the northern kingdom from the worship at Jerusalem. He was insecure because he felt that a reunion may lead to both the loss of his life and of the northern kingdom to Rehoboam, so he created a new religion and a place of worship at Bethel instead of Jerusalem (1 Kings 12:25-33). Later, when Omri became the king of the northern kingdom, he built the city of Samaria, and made it his capital, that is, the capital of the Northern Kingdom. In his reign, Ahab - Omri's son and husband of Jezebel, built a place of worship (temple) and an altar for sacrifices to Baal (1 Kings 16:24-34).

Around 722 B.C.E., Samaria and the northern kingdom of Israel was defeated by the Assyrians. The Israelites were then displaced and replaced with foreigners who worshipped other gods (2 Kings 17:23-24). As these foreigners began intermarrying with the Israelites who were left, the religion of the Jews was mixed with idolatry. Another consequence of this inter-marriage was the birth of a mixed race, something devout Jews consider as repulsive and inappropriate (see Ezra 9 and 10; Nehemiah 13:3, 23-29). Even during the time of Jesus, the Jews still harboured similar hatred for mixed race Jews. They had no dealings with them and regarded them as sinners.

The Woman of Samaria

Hopefully, the little back-story above helps you better appreciate the Samaritan woman's situation. Not only did she originate from a people whom the Jews regarded as unholy, she had had five husbands and was cohabiting with someone she wasn't married to. So, both ethically and religiously she could be considered to have missed the mark big time. Undeniably, she was a wedding champ. For someone to have had five husbands she would have had five successful weddings. I wonder how she felt in each of them. Was she joyful? Was she sad? Was she indifferent like nothing had happened?

I imagine that she was to stage one of those weddings today, her biggest fear would likely be that moment when the officiating minister declares 'Should anyone present know of any reason that this couple should not be joined in holy matrimony, speak now or forever hold your peace'. What if any of her former husbands showed up? Even if they had not come intending to cause any troubles, it would not make their presence any easier for her to handle.

At a time when some of her peers may not have tasted marriage for the first time, this woman had experienced five marital relationships and was still in the ring. How come getting men was not a problem but staying with one was? What went wrong, and who was to blame? What could we say was responsible for all her broken marriages? Or was she just unlucky with men? She was just as good at getting married as she was at losing the acclaimed 'love of her life'. Anyone who has been married multiple times will certainly have bitter stories, experiences and regrets. It is logical to expect that after her 2nd, 3rd or 4th separation, she would get so disillusioned with marriage and quit everything that had to do with men, but this wasn't so. Instead in this story we see a woman who wasn't ready to give up; it seemed she would sooner take another step in the wrong direction than not take any step at all. It appears that with each failed marriage she probably thought she had learned enough lessons to help her in the next. With her 'I can handle it' mindset, after being a wife she was now taking up the humiliating position of a girlfriend. The big constant in her life was 'Men'. It was as if she couldn't do without one; she would prefer to make do with anyone that came by, than not have a man at all.

In the day she lived in, women didn't have the freedom to work and do a lot of things. Almost everything was done by men. As such, any woman who was separated from her husband may as well be separated from life itself. Marriage meant more than just a union, it meant security, safety, provision and much more. Although women have far more liberty today compared to the past, still a woman's adoration and admiration for a union with the opposite sex appears to be something she can't help. Just like humans need water to survive, both women and men truly need each other.

The times may have changed but many people have not. Some men still treat women like trash. And a good number of women still remain vulnerable; their need to be loved, appreciated and cherished by men has held them down in abusive relationships. Marriage usually results from two people recognising their need for each other and often ends as a result of one or both parties' inability to satisfy these needs. The woman of Samaria was no different, she went through a lot to find love but now she was lost, unable to find enough courage to hold on, yet bankrupt of the necessary will to let go.

.

3
THE THIRSTY WOMAN

The woman of Samaria was as thirsty in body as in her soul and spirit. For her physical and emotional needs she knew how to find a well or a man, but deep down was a thirst which none of these things could reach or quench. Do humans truly know what they need? And if humans eventually find out what they need, will they be able to meet that need by themselves? We will answer this question shortly. In a sense, the Samaritan woman mirrors humankind, with her physical and emotional needs remaining insatiable despite several attempts to satisfy it. God has placed the need for him within every man. The only people who ever find true satisfaction and rest from their desperate search to meet their needs, find it in God alone.

Acts 17:26-27

26 And hath made of one blood all nations of men for to dwell on all the face of the Earth, and hath determined the times before appointed, and the bounds of their habitation;

27 THAT THEY SHOULD SEEK THE LORD, if haply they might feel after him, and find him, though he be not far from every one of us:

The Greek word used here for the 'seek' is 'zeteo', it means to seek, desire, crave etc. God created us with a desire, a craving for him. Nothing else can satisfy this desire but God. God has placed the desire for him in everyone. There's an inner craving in all mankind which nothing else will satisfy; it's the desire for an intimate, personal and deep relationship with God. No one can be truly satisfied, if inward satisfaction has not been achieved. The craving and desire for a deep, personal and intimate relationship with God can only be satisfied with and by God. The void and emptiness humans feel was designed by God to make us seek him; we all have a desire to connect to God but not everyone has accepted this reality.

When fulfilled, the desire to connect to God as father, gives humans their greatest satisfaction. Many being ignorant of how to satisfy this desire, go about trying to find satisfaction in all the wrong places. They end up experimenting with what was created instead of resting in the loving arms of the creator himself. Deriving satisfaction from creation only leaves one more desperately in need of the creator.

Colossians 2:9-10 (MSG)

> *9 Everything of God gets expressed in him, so you can see and hear him clearly. You don't need a telescope, a microscope, or a horoscope to realise the fullness of Christ and the emptiness of the universe without him.*
>
> *10 When you come to him, that fullness comes together for you, too. His power extends over everything.*

Searching For The Right Thing In All The Wrong Places

The craving for things with the aim of finding peace in and deriving satisfaction from them, has been the bane of human society. Physical things are not bad in themselves, they indeed provide some level of satisfaction but only for a while. Some people, thinking they can replace their need for a relationship with God with physical things, live their lives constantly trying to acquire more stuff. For many, this illusion has ultimately resulted in addiction, depression, worry, fear and anxiety, suicide and early death. The world is changing, technology is speeding up globalisation. Mankind has managed to change almost everything around it but itself. The task to change man from within supersedes the reach of man and all his technologies. Rather these technologies expose how empty man's life is without a deep, personal and intimate relationship with God. There are some things you or others will introduce to your life that could look like a good substitute for God, yet, we are complete only in him.

Colossians 2:10

> *And YE ARE COMPLETE IN HIM, which is the head of all principality and power.*

The most important need of a person is not marriage. When you have not found love in Christ, you will stumble in your love relationships with people. Thus before a person enters into a love relationship with another, he or she needs to first get into a relationship with God. Even marriage doesn't make us complete; only Jesus does.

She Wasn't Loose; She Was Lost

This is not a book for women. It's a book for everyone. It describes the situation we all find ourselves in without Jesus. Without Jesus, we may move from one thing to another searching for satisfaction and never find it. The Samaritan woman, like many today, had confused her need for the Saviour with the need for a man. But like people eventually find out, sex won't do, money won't do, fame won't do, a job won't do, friends won't do, family won't do, and power won't do; only Jesus truly fully satisfies. Sometimes it may feel like you are finally getting close to what you desire, if this fulfilment is outside Jesus though, you are only being set up for a stronger sense of dissatisfaction. This is a persistent desire that can never be substituted by anything else. If there was a man who could meet her need, the Samaritan woman certainly would have found him among the six men in her life. Is it not amusing when people think that if they change everything around them, then they will be fine? To them, everything or everyone else appears to be the problem, not them. This woman must have changed a lot of things about herself hoping that this will bring her the satisfaction she craved. Her efforts however were met with frustration. A lot of things about her were also changing. For instance, she was growing older age-wise, but she was the same in her mistakes.

Was she loose (promiscuous)? From what we can tell, she does come across as loose. But beyond being loose, she was lost! The bible makes it clear that sinful actions are not the real problem, they are only symptoms of a deeper problem - the sin nature. People do not become sinners because of their actions but because of a blood-tie to Adam, the ancestor of all mankind.

Romans 5:12

Wherefore, as by one man sin entered into the world, and death by sin; and so death passed upon all men, for that all have sinned:

The word 'sin' (Hamartia in Greek) used twice in the above verse is a noun, while the word 'sinned' (translated as Hamartano in Greek) is a verb. It is clear then, that God has declared all humankind to be sinners, not by their action but by nature. You don't become a sinner because you sinned, before you sinned you were already a sinner, sinful actions are simply an output of your sin nature.

Therefore we can conclude that the Samaritan woman wasn't loose, she was lost! Trying to change her behaviour without changing her nature would be counterproductive, but if her nature changed then her behaviour would line up as well. Her actions were not a sufficient basis to correctly define her, only her nature could truly define her. This woman was first a sinner by nature before she began committing sin. Consider this: even if you can, and do choose to start barking, you don't become a dog. However, if you were a dog, barking would be a normal action because of your nature. Some people believe all they need is to make a resolution to stop doing what is wrong and start doing what is right. Yet, after a while they find themselves back at what they solidly resolved to never do again. A person can decide not to bark again, but a dog cannot. Regardless of how many resolutions the dog makes, he will end up barking over and again. The dog's problem is not in his actions but in his nature; dog is who he is, barking is what he does. Similarly, sin is the default nature of a person long before he commits any sin. Please note, the dog analysis is for illustration purposes only.

When we say of people 'this one is loose' or 'this is an addict', we are describing them from the physical, on the basis of their actions. The spiritual reality is that they are lost (spiritually separated from God). This is true for everyone who is not born again. Becoming born-again changes your nature. In an instant you cease to be a descendant of Adam and you become a son of God. This is the only permanent solution to the sin problem. If you can change the nature of the dog for instance, you will succeed in changing his actions. However, when a person who is born again still struggles with sin, it is no longer a nature problem but one of ignorance. His nature has changed but his mind hasn't changed.

Romans 6:

5 For if we have been planted together in the likeness of his death, we shall be also in the likeness of his resurrection:

6 Knowing this, that our old man is crucified with him, that the body of sin might be destroyed, that henceforth we should not serve sin.

7 For he that is dead is freed from sin.

Mark the word 'knowing' in verse 6. It is this knowing that makes all the difference. Once you know something rightly, it will change your actions.

4

THE ROOT OF MANKIND'S STRUGGLES

I would like to show you a little more about the root of mankind's problem. In the story of creation, the Bible tells us that after God made everything, he saw that it was good.

Genesis 1:31
> *And God saw everything that he has made, and behold, it was very good.*

Some people accuse God for being irresponsible or directly responsible for all the problems of the human race, this is usually a question of his 'omnipotence'. "If he is really a powerful God, why can't he stop the death of babies, wars, hurricanes and other natural disasters?" people have asked. Everything he created is in a mess and he is doing nothing about it?"

Religion has tried to present an answer to these questions by replying that sickness, death and natural disasters are some of God's ways to punish us for the sins we have committed or his way to teach us life lessons. Religion also claims that God uses the problems of life to bring us closer to himself. Interestingly, many of the people who say such will never use evil things to hurt their kids, yet they believe God does so to his children. Religious people are not bad. I believe they mean well in the way they talk about God but their faulty presentation of him is causing disaster! Trying to draw people closer to God without focusing on Jesus will only achieve the opposite effect; rather than coming to God, they will end up running from him.

The representation of God as the one who controls whatever happens on Earth, is one reason why many have become atheists. This lie has also made some believers erroneously accept what the devil does, as the work of God. They accept sickness, poverty and death, believing that God wants to take the glory or that he wants to teach them humility. With all this chaos in our world, it is illogical to affirm that an 'Omnipotent God' who is popularly referred to as 'good' is running this Earth. The Bible clearly shows us that God did not just make a 'good' creation, he called his creation 'very good'. What went wrong then, what happened to the very good creation?

Genesis 1:26

> *And God said, let us make man in our image, after our likeness: And let them have dominion over the fish of the sea, and over the fowl of the air, and over the cattle, and over all the Earth, and over every creeping thing that creepeth upon the Earth.*

From this scripture we see that God made man to exercise dominion over the Earth. God did not create him to be a figurehead or a puppet so God could continue to call the shots, he created the Earth for man to run things. Man was given the power to determine what happens on Earth. Another scripture illustrates this:

Genesis 2: 15-17

> *15 And the Lord God took the man, and put him in the garden of Eden to dress and keep it.*
> *16 And the Lord God commanded the man, saying, of every tree of the garden thou mayest freely eat :*
> *17 But of the tree of knowledge of Good and Evil, thou shall not eat of it: for in the day that that eatest thereof thou shalt surely die.*

Psalm 115: 16

> *The heaven, even the heavens, are the LORD'S: but the Earth hath he given to the children of men.*

If God is in charge of this Earth then he lied in the verse above. When you handover something to someone, you are no longer in charge nor expected to interfere unless the new owner invites you to do so. Power and authority was given to man, whatever happened on Earth was within man's jurisdiction. In essence, humans are to be held responsible for whatever happens around them, whether good or bad.

Man's Rebellion is the Cause of His Problems

God cannot be rightfully accused of being an irresponsible creator or for not properly managing what he has created. The problem man has found himself in is a result of his decision to cede the power that was given to him, to the devil.

Genesis 3: 4-5

> *4 And the Serpent said unto the woman, ye shall not surely die:*
> *5 For God doth know that in the day ye eat thereof, then your eyes shall be opened, and you shall be as gods, knowing Good and Evil.*

6 And when the woman saw that the tree was good for food, and that it was pleasant to the eyes, and a tree to be desired to make one wise, she took of the fruit thereof, and did eat, And gave also unto her husband with her: and he did eat.

7 And the eyes of them both were opened and they knew that they were naked: And sewed fig leaves together, and made themselves aprons.

Chapter one in the book of Genesis already told us that God made man in his image and likeness. In chapter two, we are told that Adam, the first man, was told not to eat from the tree of the knowledge of Good and Evil. This suggests that he had free will. He had the ability to make decisions on his own, otherwise it would have been useless to instruct him not to eat from the forbidden tree if he could only do whatever he had been programmed to do. The devil came along in chapter three and sold the idea to Eve that there was something she needed to do, to be like God. In other words, he was telling her that she was not yet the image and likeness of God. Clearly, he was lying. The devil knew that if he could make man commit sin by eating from the tree of the knowledge of good and evil, then the power over the Earth would become his.

A lot of times I've been asked 'why did God create the tree in the first place if he didn't want man to eat it?' Someone has also asked me 'why did he not stop them from eating it?' Well, neither the existence of that tree nor God's refusal to infringe on man's free will is the issue. To prove this, let's see what the scripture has to say.

1st Timothy 2:13 - 14

For Adam was first formed, then Eve. And Adam was not deceived, but the woman being deceived was in the transgression.

30

Eve was deceived, but the man, Adam, whom God put in charge of the Earth was not deceived. The tree being there or not is not the issue, because man was not destined to eat it, nor did God plant it there to tempt man. The existence of the tree was rather proof that man indeed had free will. By what Adam did, he outrightly ceded the power over the Earth to the devil. It was not a case of deception, Adam used his freewill to make a terrible decision. If God had burst out of the blue thundering 'Adam no, don't eat that fruit!', his interference would mean Adam was not really in charge, that he could not choose for himself. This would imply that God lied when he said he gave man dominion, since man couldn't be allowed to make his own decisions. The fall of Adam shows us that man really had power. He could decide by his will what he wanted and do it without interference. Let's see another scripture.

Luke 4:

> *5 And the devil, taking him up into a high mountain, shewed unto him, all the Kingdoms of the world in a moment of time.*
> *6 And the devil said unto him, all this power will I give thee, and the glory of them: For that is delivered unto me, and to whosoever I will I give it.*
> *7 If thou therefore will worship me, all shall be thine.*

Did you observe that the devil said the power was 'delivered to him'? he didn't claim to have created the power. And he was certainly not bluffing about having power, otherwise this could not have been a real temptation. This power that was delivered to him was the very power that God gave to Adam. The problems many blame God for is simply the consequence of man's poor decision in the garden and his corresponding loss of control over this Earth. Adam gave the devil influence over all creation the moment he wilfully ceded the power God entrusted him with, to the devil. God had nothing to do with it. As a result of this fall, all mankind became children of the devil by nature, and all creations were removed from under his control. The human race has lost control over this world and the devil has become the god of this world.

2nd Corinthians 4:4

> *In whom THE GOD OF THIS WORLD hath blinded the minds of them which believe not, lest the light of the glorious gospel of Christ, who is the image of God, should shine unto them.*

Adam's rebellion made him lose control over the Earth. Today all mankind and the whole of creation are suffering from Adam's wrong decision. God is not to blame for all this; he doesn't have a hand in the chaos going on all over the world.

The Problem Outside Man Is A Manifestation Of The Spiritual Death That Has Happened Inside

Genesis 2:17

> *But of the tree of the knowledge of good and evil, thou shalt not eat of it: FOR IN THE DAY THAT THOU EATEST THEREOF THOU SHALT SURELY DIE.*

When God said man will die if he eats from that tree of the knowledge of good and evil, it wasn't a joke. Man died after eating the fruit, not only a physical death but a spiritual one as well. After the fall, Adam and Eve sure didn't look like dead men, lying down flat in the state of rigor mortis. They were very much alive physically; talking, walking and seeing, yet death had already happened within them. First we see that something happened to them; they became ashamed, naked and afraid to stand before God.

Even after they had sewn fig leaves, they still went into hiding when they heard the voice of God. This shows that whatever went wrong was farther than clothes could handle and deeper than eyes could see. On the surface level, everything appeared good but it can be seen that what happened to the duo was more than physical. The leaves they sewed could not deal with all the problems, covering themselves on the outside alone didn't get to the root of the problem either. A man and his wife were alone in the garden yet they were ashamed. The death they were warned about had happened within them, the shame and guilt they were now experiencing, were only a physical manifestation of this death. There are three types of death mentioned in the bible.

a. Physical Death is the situation where the human spirit separates from his body.

James 2:26
> *For as the BODY WITHOUT THE SPIRIT IS DEAD...*

b. Spiritual Death refers to the situation where the Spirit of man is separated from God.

Ephesians 2:1.
> *And you had he quickened, who were dead in trespasses and sins;*

Ephesians 2:12
> *That at that time ye were without Christ, being aliens from the commonwealth of israel, and strangers from the Covenant of promise, having no hope and WITHOUT GOD IN THE WORLD*

Paul in these verses describes the spiritual condition of these people before they were saved. He wasn't referring to physical death, because the people whom Apostle Paul was writing to were alive. No one in his right senses will write a letter for dead people to read. Paul said they were 'dead in trespasses and sins', and in another place he said they were 'without God in this world'. This death was in their spirit, they were spiritually separated from God. In yet another instance, while talking to the Ephesians in this same epistle Paul said:

Ephesians 4: 17-18
17 This I say therefore, and testify in the Lord, that ye henceforth work not as other gentiles walk, in the vanity of their mind,
18 Having the understanding darkened, BEING ALIENATED FROM THE LIFE OF GOD...

From this verse we can see that the scripture explains spiritual death as being separated from the life of God. Anything separated from life is dead. So, being disconnected from God means more than separation, it means death. This is the true condition of all those who are not saved; they are spiritually dead, they are devoid of God's life.

John 10:10
The thief cometh not, but for to steal, and to kill, and to destroy: I AM COME THAT THEY MIGHT HAVE LIFE, AND THAT THEY MIGHT HAVE IT MORE ABUNDANTLY.

Jesus came so that we might have life. He came to put an end to the death in our spirit that occurred due to our separation from God. He has reconciled us to God through his death. When we receive Jesus, we receive life into our spirit. He has brought us near to God, there is no more separation; the death that was in our spirit has been put to an end by the sacrifice of Jesus.

Ephesians 2:13

13 But now in Christ Jesus, ye who sometimes were far off are made nigh by the blood of Christ.

c. **Eternal Death** is also called the second death. It refers to being cast into the lake of fire. Eternal death is the home and future of anyone who rejects salvation by faith in Jesus Christ.

Revelation 20:14-15

14 And death and hell were cast into the lake of fire. This is the second death.

15 And whosoever was not found written in the book of life was cast into the lake of fire.

Paul, while talking about the condition of the Ephesian believers before they received Christ, said they were 'alienated'. In other words, they were disconnected from the life of God. Anyone who has not received salvation by faith in Jesus is dead in his spirit even though alive in body.

Romans 5:12

Wherefore, as by one man sin entered into the world, and death by sin; and so death passed upon all men, for that all have sinned:

The real condition the Samaritan woman had was not a physical one. If she were to describe the state of her life, she would have probably blamed XYZ as the cause of all her problems. She could have blamed witches or some ancestral curse as the reason her life was that way. But the sin and problems she was dealing with outwardly were simply a result of her inward state of death.

Mark 7:20-23

20 And he said, That which cometh out of the man, that defileth the man.

21 for from within, out of the heart of men, proceed evil thoughts, adulteries, fornications, murders,

22 thefts, covetousness, wickedness, deceit, lasciviousness, an evil eye, blasphemy, pride, foolishness:

23 All these evil things come from within, and defile the man.

The death in the human spirit shows up in different forms in a person's soul and body. When a person sins, it is an evidence of the death of their sense of good judgement or morals. Sicknesses and diseases are also manifestations of death in the human body. It is proof that man is dying outside because he has died inside. Poverty is another manifestation of death in the human soul; his intelligence and creativity can't sustain him. Divorce also shows that one's marriage is dying. The list of physical conditions as proof of spiritual death is endless.

To illustrate this, I will use the analogy of tree cutting. Immediately after cutting down a tree, its leaves remain green, everything seems normal about the tree except that it has been severed from the root. As days roll by, the tree gradually begins to physically manifest the death that has happened inside it. The moment a tree is disconnected from the sap that flows inside it from the root, it won't appear dead at once. However give it time and you will begin to see physical or outward proof of what has gone wrong inside the tree. The death that happened inwardly made man a sinner by nature. His problems on the outside are merely symptoms; the real problem is his separation from God. The problems of man started after his rebellion, there was no record of any problems till after the fall of man.

The Samaritan woman we have been talking about was fighting to change what was outside, to win the battle outside. At the same time, she was losing the battle on the inside where the real root of all her problems lay.

5

THE SATISFACTION SHE REALLY NEEDED

L et's get back to where we left off with the Samaritan woman. Her adultery and poor lifestyle choices were a manifestation of the death in her spirit. She thought she could solve this inner need with the presence of a man in her life but things only got worse. What she was trying to get from man could only be given by God. Having failed over and again, no words could describe the shame and rejection she must have felt. At this point in her life hiding her past would be of utmost importance to her. She knew that it would be difficult to find a man who would want to stay in a marital relationship with her, after knowing about all her failed marriages. The present man in her life didn't want to be committed to her as a husband. Could it be that this guy was afraid of committing his future to a woman with a track record of divorce? Maybe he was scared to pledge total devotion to a woman who was a legend in not staying married.

Her life was in such a mess. Her female friends, assuming she had any, certainly would have done their best to keep her away from their own husbands. She was a potential threat to any woman who had a man in her life. Her relations would have been ashamed to be identified with her due to the stain and shame she was bringing to their family name. Unarguably, the negative impact of her failed marriages would have taken a toll on her.

Personally, I think this woman must have been really attractive. If this was not the case, then one begins to wonder what the men in her life found special about her. However, no matter how beautiful she must have been, the beauty couldn't cover her hurt. No make-up ran deep enough to cover the pain and dissatisfaction she must have felt. The mirror told her she was beautiful, but not her hurting heart. She could hide the truth from a lot of people but not herself. There's no make-up for a hurting heart, only the love of God can get there. At the point where we meet her, the Samaritan woman was at a crossroad; she could not go back to her previous husbands, she could not find another man to marry her, and she could not leave the one who wanted a wife that he would only be a boyfriend to. He demanded full commitment yet he wanted to remain uncommitted on his part. She was trapped.

For her thirst, she knew where to find water, for her emotions she knew where to find a man, but for the true satisfaction in her spirit, she was at a loss for what to do. Whenever you find yourself struggling with the same problem over and again, it simply shows that you lack the ability to help yourself and you are really in need of help. If this is you, stop trying to help yourself, what you need is a saviour, and he knows where to find you. He loves you, he will come for you when everyone else deserts you. He knows what you really need, and only he can truly satisfy the dissatisfaction you feel inside.

Real Satisfaction

Here's the contrast of a woman who in her lifetime was married just once. When her husband died, she did not become depressed, frustrated, or promiscuous. She just lived up the rest of her life praying, fasting and ministering to the Lord. Her relationship with God seemed to fulfil her need for man.

Luke 2: 36 - 38

> *36 And there was one Anna, a prophetess, the daughter of Phanuel, of the tribe of Aser: she was of a great age, and had lived with an husband seven years from her virginity;*
>
> *37 And she was a widow of about fourscore and four years, which departed not from the temple, but served God with fastings and prayers night and day.*
>
> *38 And she coming in that instant gave thanks likewise unto the Lord, and spake of him to all them that looked for redemption in Jerusalem.*

Marriage is good but it cannot and does not bring the complete satisfaction we need. Until you are satisfied in a relationship with God, you cannot find satisfaction in any human relationship. Anyone without Christ is bankrupt of love, and going into a love relationship without having a personal relationship with Jesus will worsen the bankruptcy. It's futile to be empty of God's love and hope to find love in the arms of another human who is equally empty. An eighty four year old woman - Anna, was content with just seven years of marriage, whereas another woman was jumping from one relationship to the other, leaving behind a trail of failure. What the Samaritan woman was searching for and never found, Anna found in the arms of a loving God.

This is not to say we ought to be fasting and praying every day of our lives, but that there's a great need in our soul to have a personal relationship with God. That deep personal and intimate relationship with God is what we truly need, all other points of satisfaction must be plugged into that. Both women lived in similar times; one conformed to the pressure of life and society, the other conformed to the will of God for her. It is not God's will or design for all women to stay in church praying and fasting. If this was so then every other woman not in church (synagogue) at that time and even now could be rightfully considered a failure. The Bible also spoke about Elizabeth the mother of John the Baptist, who lived in the same time period as these two other women. She was blameless and righteous according to the law. Elizabeth stayed many years without a child of her own, yet she remained with one husband and was content.

Luke 1: 5-6

> *5 There was in the days of Herod, the king of Judea, a certain priest named Zacharias, of the course of Abia: and his wife was of the daughters of Aaron, and her name was Elisabeth.*
> *6 And they were both righteous before God, walking in all the commandments and ordinances of the Lord blameless.*

Elizabeth and Anna had one thing in common; a personal relationship with this God. Both of these ladies had knowledge of the Messiah who was to come. In God's plan, one of them was to pray until the messiah came while the other was to be the mother of the forerunner of the messiah. There is real satisfaction in knowing God and staying put where you fit in his plan. So much dissatisfaction comes from trying to fit into the lives of others, without regard for God's plan for you.

Colossians 1:16

> *For by him were all things created, that are in heaven, and that are in Earth, visible and invisible, whether they be thrones, or dominions, or principalities, or powers: ALL THINGS WERE CREATED BY HIM, AND FOR HIM:*

All things were created by him and for him, everything is his. A car is never made for itself, it is usually created with a user in mind, for someone to drive. Without someone to drive it, the car will be useless. The car is at its best not when it's parked but when it's on the move. It is only in the hands of the person for whom it was made, that a car finds real relevance. We are made for God, so without a deep, personal and intimate relationship with him, we will be like a car parked, never reaching the true essence of our existence.

A Relationship With God Based On His Grace

Exodus 19:5-6

> *5 Now therefore, if YE will obey my voice indeed, and keep my covenant, then YE shall be a peculiar people unto me above all people: for all the Earth is mine:*
> *6 And YE shall be unto me a kingdom of priests, and an holy nation. These are the words which THOU shalt speak unto the children of Isreal.*

Exodus 15:26

> *And said, if THOU will diligently hearken to the voice of the Lord thy God, and wilt do that which is right in his sight, and wilt give ear to his commandments, and keep all his status, I will put none*

of the diseases upon thee, which I have brought upon the Egyptians: for I am the Lord that healeth thee.

In the Old Testament people had a relationship with God that was based on their good works. This relationship was conditioned on one's performance, it was intact as long as you could keep the list of do's and don'ts. Under this covenant, the emphasis was on 'thou' or 'ye', which is old English for 'you'. God could be trusted to keep his own end of the deal, and we were to keep our part too otherwise evil was sure to befall us. God's goodness and mercy was dependent on the good things we could do. This covenant did not solve our need for a deep, personal and intimate relationship with God because whenever we failed the relationship ceased. People who lived in the Old Testament enjoyed some level of satisfaction based on how much they kept the laws of Moses. However, the problem was, no one had in him the ability to keep all the laws without fail because all men were by nature sinners.

Hebrew 10: 1-3

> *1 For the law having a shadow of good things to come, and not the very image of the things, can never with those sacrifices which they offered year by year continually make the comers thereunto perfect.*
> *2 For then would they not have ceased to be offered? because that the worshippers once purged should have had no more conscience of sins.*
> *3 But in those sacrifices there is a remembrance again made of sins every year.*

The temple rituals could not deal with the conscience of sin. The word translated as 'conscience' can also be translated as consciousness. The repetition of the sacrifice yearly brought the consciousness of sin. In other words, every year as the people gathered to witness the sacrifice they were reminded of their sins; the feeling of unworthiness and guilt remained. There is no ninety nine percent (99%) in keeping the law, once you failed in regards to one law, you were considered to have failed all. For the man under this covenant, his prosperity, health and well-being, safety, and all the good things he desired, was based on his faithfulness to the law. He was also to bear the cost of atonement every time he slipped. This covenant was burdensome to all. Both the rich and poor kept spending on sacrifices they knew could not completely save them; in addition to the stress of the yearly sacrifice, the conscience of sin was always present.

Thank God the new covenant does not work that way, it is not based on anything we do. We can be sure of health, blessings, prosperity and so much more, simply because of Jesus. And unlike the old covenant with its 'thou/ye' emphasis, this new covenant based on God's unconditional love for us, is full of 'I will'.

Hebrews 8: 10-12
> *10 For this is the covenant that I WILL make with the house of Isreal after those days, saith the Lord: I WILL put my laws into their mind, and write them in their hearts: and I WILL be to them a God, and they shall be to me a people:*
> *11 And they shall not teach every man his neighbor, and every man his brother, saying, know the Lord: for all shall know me, from the least to the greatest.*
> *12 For I WILL be merciful to their unrighteousness, and their sins and their iniquities WILL I remember no more.*

The Samaritan woman was in dire need of a relationship with God but she was completely disqualified from it based on her way of life, being a sinner by nature and a Samaritan. If ever she would have a relationship with God, it

THE WELL, THE WOMAN, AND THE WONDERFUL SAVIOUR

would have to be by his grace. Jesus came for this very reason; to satisfy our need for a relationship with God based on his grace (unconditional favour). He took the burden of living up to all God's laws and he died for us to have God's grace. Since we didn't qualify for this grace, we cannot be disqualified from it; we can only decide to reject it.

PART 3:
THE SAVIOUR

THE SAVIOUR

When man sinned in the Garden of Eden, he was doomed to face the consequences of his action. The penalty for the sin that man has committed was death. The Bible says that Heaven and Earth will pass away but the word of God will surely come to pass.

Romans 5: 12-14

12 Wherefore, as by one man sin entered into the world, and death by sin; and so death passed upon all men, FOR THAT ALL HAVE SINNED:

14 Nevertheless DEATH REIGNED FROM ADAM TO MOSES, EVEN OVER THEM THAT HAD NOT SINNED AFTER THE SIMILITUDE OF ADAM'S TRANSGRESSION, who is the figure of him that was to come.

The Bible says for all have sinned. In God's sight, the entire human race has sinned. The fate and the future of mankind was in the hands of Adam to decide, and his decision in that garden became the fate of all his children. Even though we were not physically present in the garden, all mankind had the same judgement as Adam so long as they were from his lineage, i.e they had been born human. The death God spoke about in the garden wasn't a physical one. He was referring to spiritual death. As I have established earlier, you could see physically speaking, Adam was well and alive after the disobedience, he continued to exhibit all characteristics of living things.

The fact that all humans today die, however, confirms that the judgement of Adam's sin is upon his offspring. And apart from the physical death and spiritual death, eternal death awaits all mankind. God did not place a death sentence on man, rather God placed a death sentence as the penalty for sin. When man sinned he brought that death sentence upon himself. Death is the reward for taking sides with sin.

Because of the sin of Adam, all mankind would surely face the same future as the devil who has been doomed to eternal death in the lake of fire. Man was in a desperate need of a saviour but who would this Saviour be? Or could we save ourselves? Obviously not. If man dared to step from time into eternity without a saviour he would be doomed, so, the saviour stepped out of eternity into time so he could save man.

Matthew 1: 21.

And she shall bring forth a son, and also called his name Jesus: For he shall SAVE his people from their sins.

John 1:29.

The next day John seeth Jesus coming unto him and saith, behold the lamb of God, which TAKETH AWAY the sin of the world.

First John 2:2

And he is the PROPITIATION for our sins: And not for us only, but also for the sin of the whole world.

6.
WHO IS THE SAVIOUR?

A. He Is The Son Of God

John 3: 16-17

16 For God so loved the world, that he gave his only begotten son, that whosoever believeth in him should not perish, but have everlasting life.

17 FOR GOD SENT NOT HIS SON INTO THE WORLD to condemn the world; but that the world THROUGH HIM might be SAVED.

B. He Is Sinless

Looking at what the scripture says, we can see that no man born from the union of a man and a woman could have saved mankind, because everyone who came into this world as a result of the union between a man and his wife, entered in with Adam's death sentence hanging over their head. And of course a criminal cannot save another criminal, only a righteous man can.

Psalms 49: 7 -15

> *7 NONE OF THEM CAN BY ANY MEANS REDEEM HIS BROTHER, NOR GIVE TO GOD A RANSOM FOR HIM:*
>
> *8 (FOR THE REDEMPTION OF THEIR SOUL IS PRECIOUS, and it ceaseth forever:) that he should still live forever, and not see corruption.*
>
> *15 But God will redeem my soul from the power of the grave: For he shall receive me. Salah.*

In the context of this verse above, the redemption of their soul being precious meant that it was far more than human riches or wealth could purchase. Something precious - more valuable than money, would be needed for the redemption of man.

1st Peter 1: 18 -19

> *18 Forasmuch as ye know that ye were not redeemed with corruptible things, as silver and gold, from your vain conversation received by traditions from your fathers;*
>
> *19 But with the PRECIOUS BLOOD OF CHRIST, AS OF A LAMB WITHOUT BLEMISH AND WITHOUT SPOT:*

Sin made it impossible for anyone with the seed of Adam to be the redeemer of the entire human race. Since sin had been passed down to all humankind and all were sinners. In order to save mankind, the saviour would have to be a man without the sin nature of Adam. A spirit could not bear man's death sentence because spirits don't die. All men were doomed to die, only a man who wasn't under this sentence couldn't bring others out from it. Jesus came as a man to bear that death sentence.

1st Corinthians 15:21

> *For since by man came death, by man came also the resurrection of the dead.*

The blood of Jesus was precious because it had no connection with Adam's life. Blood represents life, thus when Jesus shed his blood on the cross, he in essence gave his life for us. A man with a death sentence on himself cannot save another man who has the same fate as him. The only way a criminal can save himself or another criminal is by committing another crime, thereby worsening the case. If we could save ourselves or someone else could save us, Jesus would not have come. He came because only he can save us and no one else. If he hadn't saved us, we all would have still been doomed.

C. He Is The Seed Of The Woman

Genesis 3:15

> *And I will put enmity between thee and the woman, and between thy seed and HER SEED; it shall bruise thy head, and thou shalt bruise his heel.*

Luke 1:

> *30 And the angel said unto her, fear not Mary: for thou hast found favour with God.*
>
> *31 And, Behold, thou shalt conceive in thy womb, and bring forth a son, and shalt call his name Jesus.*
>
> *34 Then said Mary unto the angel, how shall this be, seeing I know not a man?*
>
> *35 And the angel answered and said unto her, the Holy Ghost shall come upon thee, and the power of the Highest shall overshadow*

thee: therefore also that holy thing which shall be born of thee shall be called the son of God.

Matthew 1:23

Behold, a virgin shall be with child, and shall bring forth a son, and they shall call his name Emmanuel, which being interpreted is, God with us.

Jesus was born without the life of Adam. God took from the woman's seed (egg) and made Jesus without any contribution from a man (husband). When she asked how this would be possible, the angel said to Mary, 'the Holy Ghost shall come upon thee, and the power of the Highest shall overshadow thee'. The Holy Spirit is the one who made Jesus' conception possible. An egg was therefore fertilised without a sperm; Jesus was born without any contribution of a man. One of the physiological functions of the placenta is to ensure that the blood of the baby and the mother never mixes. So, Jesus didn't receive Adam's life (blood) from either his father or mother. Jesus didn't have the sin nature in him because he didn't get his life from man.

Leviticus 17:11

FOR THE LIFE OF THE FLESH IS IN THE BLOOD: and I have given it to you upon the altar to make an atonement for your souls: for it is the blood that maketh an atonement for the soul.

D. He Was Made Sin

2nd Corinthians 5:21

For HE HATH MADE HIM TO BE SIN FOR US, WHO KNEW NO SIN; that we might be made the righteousness of God in him.

Jesus could save us because he himself was sinless. He did not have the life of Adam in him nor did he have any personal debt of sin or death to clear up. As a result, he could bear the sin penalty for all. People sometimes act as though there is something they can do to be saved. If there was anything man could do to earn his salvation, Jesus wouldn't have come. He came because man was doomed to die, the fate and future of man was hell due to his rebellion against God.

God is a just God, yet he is equally a loving father and therein was the dilemma. He couldn't go back on his words or change the law to state that the wages of sin is no longer death, nor would he stop loving man due to sin. As a just God he must see to it that sin was punished, but as a loving father he must also ensure the sinner was shown grace in Christ Jesus. By the death of Jesus on the cross, God perfectly resolved the crisis. Face to face with damnation, man found himself stuck; he could not remove his sin nature, he could not go back to undo his sinful actions, yet he could not go forward to face the consequences of his sin. But in-between man and eternal death, the saviour showed up. He faced death for man and the judgement of God was satisfied. The saviour did not just die for all mankind, he died as mankind. Since Jesus died for all of us, then we were all included in his death, and because he died as us, we can claim his death as the payment for our sin.

2nd Corinthians 5:14.

For the love of Christ constraineth us; because we thus judge, that IF ONE DIED FOR ALL, THEN WERE ALL DEAD:

7

THE SAVIOUR REACHED FOR US WHEN WE COULDN'T
REACH HIM

Jesus began his conversation with the woman, using what she could relate with. He approached her from an angle she could understand, coming down to her level rather than attempting to bring her to his level.

John 4:7

> *...Jesus said to the woman, give me drink*

No matter who you are or what you have done, Jesus knows how to relate with you. He knows exactly what you need and he is reaching out for you. The saviour did not come to condemn the sinner but to save them. Jesus came both to save you from your sin, and to help you end all the fruitless efforts of trying to relate with your heavenly father without any sense of fear, guilt, shame and condemnation.

The Saviour Has You In Mind

Back to our story. Jesus came to Samaria deliberately. The Bible says, 'he must needs go through Samaria', so the Samaritan woman was on his mind. This woman, as we have earlier seen, did nothing to deserve this gesture. Thank God, our Saviour does not come to anyone because of how good they are, but because of how good he is. He did not hide himself and wait for the woman to find him. He came to the exact place where he knew he could find her. He didn't start towards her and then stop halfway through, expecting the woman to find him; he came to find the woman and went all the way to do so. Just in case you are lost in sin, you may not know where to find Jesus but he knows where you are. And like the Samaritan woman, you won't get to the well and need to wait for him, he's already there waiting for you. He's at the point of your need. Salvation is now available because he loves you.

He Loves You Personally

The women in Samaria may have been judged to be of better character or morals; compared to this woman they were good, but compared to the saviour, they all had the same fate as her. Compared to other people we may score ourselves good, but compared to God we don't stand a chance of ever coming close to the standard of his holiness. Of all the women who lived in Samaria, the Saviour chose to meet this woman. He got to the well before her, waited till she came and was the first to initiate a discussion. Jesus takes you personally. If he could search for this woman who wasn't qualified, you don't need to bother about qualifying for his love. He loves and his love qualifies you.

There was nothing good she did to earn this encounter. She was not qualified religiously, she was not qualified ethically, and as a matter of fact, religion and ethics do not qualify us to receive anything from God. If they could, God would have set the religious rules and ethical standards that would bring us salvation when we meet their requirements. But because laws and ethics could not save, God had to send his son. There is nothing anyone can do that can save, only Jesus can save.

Jesus is completely gracious. He has not come half way expecting you to complete the remaining distance. He went all the way for this woman who wasn't qualified. He got there before she arrived and patiently waited for however long it took her to arrive, without getting tired or resentful. He didn't immediately go all prophetic on her, to point out her faults and rub it in her face, rather, the saviour spoke to her as someone who had no questions to answer, as one whose past did not exist.

Many times we are so concerned about our qualifications but God doesn't care about that, he has qualified those he cares about! He has brought them to share in his nature and glory. Whatever he has can now be accessed by them because of the finished work of Christ. We are now sons of God because of his grace.

He Stepped Out Before You

The woman may have been cold-footed, taking her time as she went towards the well that day, yet Jesus was there, patiently waiting. No one is too sinful for him to accept. He came all the way, not for religious people but for sinners. Jesus came to save you. He didn't come to condemn the sinner but to condemn sin. The sinner is not God's enemy, sin is. Because any sinner who steps out of time into eternity is doomed, the saviour stepped out of eternity into time to save them. This is too good to be true.

John 4:9

Then saith the woman of Samaria unto him, HOW IS IT THAT

THOU, BEING A JEW, ASKEST DRINK OF ME, which am a woman of Samaria? for the Jews have no dealings with the Samaritans.

This woman was puzzled, quickly she had to remind this stranger that he stood a chance of making himself unclean by this interaction with her. She couldn't understand why this man being a Jew would stoop so low as to have anything to do with her. Little did she know the man she was talking to was not just a Jew, he was Jesus the saviour himself. Usually, when a religious person is reminded of the prospects of becoming unclean by coming in contact with a Samaritan or sinner, he will instantly draw back. Jesus however continued to interact with this woman. In essence he was saying 'talking to you was not a mistake, I chose to. I am not here to condemn you, I'm here because I love you'. The name 'Jesus' means saviour. He is not one you can stain with sin but the one who can save you from the stains of sin. No sinner ever comes in contact with Jesus and remains unclean. Our sin doesn't change his attitude towards us. Our sin doesn't change his love towards us, rather his love changes us.

Salvation Is Courtesy Of His Grace

Ephesians 2:8

> *For by grace are ye saved through faith; and that not of yourselves: it is the gift of God:*

Ephesians 2:8 (NLT)

> *GOD SAVED YOU BY HIS GRACE WHEN YOU BELIEVED. AND YOU CAN'T TAKE CREDIT FOR THIS; IT IS A GIFT FROM GOD.*

You can't take credit for salvation, from start to finish God covered the distance. He was waiting for you even before you took the first step. You might argue 'but I had faith, I was the one who believed'. True, you had to do the believing, you had to proclaim your faith in Jesus, but even the believing was a gift from him to you.

Ephesians 2:8 (LB)
> *Because of his kindness, you have been saved through trusting Christ. AND EVEN TRUSTING IS NOT OF YOURSELVES; IT TOO IS A GIFT FROM GOD.*

The knowledge of God's kindness imparted you and caused faith to rise in your heart. There's nothing you contributed to your salvation; from start to finish God covered the cost. Your salvation is courtesy of his grace.

The Greatest I Love You

Jesus got to the well wearied with his journey according to John 4 verse 7. He went all the way there not in his private jet but on his 'private shoes'. He went on foot, thirsty and hungry at about the 6th hour or 12 noon, which is when the sun is usually hottest. Why did Jesus come under this severe condition? Because of the woman! Yes, because of YOU!

Hebrew 2:14 -18
> *14 For as much then as the children are partakers of flesh and blood, he also himself likewise took part of the same; that through death he might destroy him that had the power of death, that is, the devil;*
> *15 And deliver them who through fear of death were all their lifetime subject to bondage.*
> *16 For verily he took not on him the nature of angels; but he took on him the seed of Abraham.*

17 Wherefore in all things it behoved him to be made like unto his brethren, that he might be a merciful and faithful high priest in things pertaining to God, to make reconciliation for the sins of the people.

18 For in that he himself hath suffered being tempted, he is able to succour them that are tempted.

8

THE LIVING WATER

His willingness to connect with you beats your willingness to connect with him. In this conversation, Jesus showed that he wanted to give, not take from the woman. It is so empowering to rest in this knowledge that we have a 'giving saviour'. This is who Jesus is, even on the cross, he showed his love for us by giving his life for us.

John 4:10

> *Jesus answered and said unto her, If thou knewest the gift of God, and who it is that saith to thee, Give me to drink; thou wouldest have asked of him, and he would have given thee living water.*

Deuteronomy 10:20

> *THOU SHALT FEAR THE LORD THY GOD; him shalt thou serve, and to him shalt thou cleave, and swear by his name.*

In the Old Testament when Moses said 'thou shalt fear the lord thy God' he spoke about the fear of God. In the New Testament however, Jesus referring to this statement of Moses showed us that this fear of God is 'reverence'. Our Saviour didn't come to demand unconditional obedience to the law as the condition for us to receive anything from God. He came primarily to give us the gift of himself, not the gift of things.

He Did Not Come To Take, He Came To Give

John 4:10 - 14

> *10 Jesus answered and said unto her, If thou knewest the gift of God, and who it is that saith to thee, Give me to drink; THOU WOULDEST HAVE ASKED OF HIM, and HE WOULD HAVE GIVEN THEE LIVING WATER.*
>
> *11 The woman saith unto him, Sir, thou hast nothing to draw with, and the well is deep: from whence then hast thou that living water?*
>
> *12 Art thou greater than our father Jacob, which gave us the well, and drank thereof himself, and his children, and his cattle?*
>
> *13 Jesus answered and said unto her, Whosoever drinketh of this water shall thirst again:*
>
> *14 BUT WHOSOEVER DRINKETH OF THE WATER THAT I SHALL GIVE HIM SHALL NEVER THIRST; but the water that I shall give him shall be in him a well of water springing up into everlasting life.*

His love is what leads us to repentance. His love is what makes us revere him. Some people think that the more you show sinners the ten commandments and all the punishments that will befall them when they fall short of it, they will have the fear of God and stop sinning. This assumption is far from the truth. It is only when people feel loved by God that they can truly reverence him.

Psalm 130:3-4

> *3 If thou, LORD, shouldest mark iniquities, O Lord, who shall stand?*
> *4 BUT THERE IS FORGIVENESS WITH THEE, THAT THOU MAYEST BE FEARED.*

The word 'fear' in this verse is from a Hebrew word 'yare' which is translated as 'reverence, respect, honor, fear and dreadful'. How do we know which word will best express the message in this verse?

Matthew 4:10

> *Then saith Jesus unto him, get thee hence, satan: for it is written, THOU SHALT WORSHIP the lord thy God, and him only shalt thou serve.*

From the words of Jesus in the verse above, we see what the fear of God is. It is worship. The word 'worship' in this verse is translated from a Greek word 'proskuneo', which means 'to reverence'. In verse 11 of John 4, we see that the Samaritan woman called Jesus 'Lord', when she saw his love. The Greek word 'kurios' was translated as 'sir' in this verse. It means 'Lord, Owner, Master, God'. As their discussion proceeded, the Samaritan woman continued to refer to him as 'Sir'. The conversation had seemingly begun with little or no reverence or respect, but now the woman was naturally reverencing; showing some respect by calling him 'Sir'.

Her first word to him had been 'how can you being a Jew...', now she was referring to him as 'Sir'. She must have noticed the difference between this stranger and other Jews she had met. She may have perceived that this man was a good person who didn't mind coming close to her. She figured out that this man as a Jew had put his status and reputation on the line just to talk to her, not minding the risk of becoming unclean. In view of all these, she began to revere him. At this point she didn't know that the person she was talking to was the messiah, yet she had become better in her response to him because of the kindness and love he showed towards her.

When we present God accurately as the gracious and loving father that he is, we will see more souls saved effortlessly. When we put before sinners a faulty presentation of God, we will surely scare them away. Oftentimes, our evangelism could often be rendered ineffective if our words, approach and presence bring a sense of condemnation to unbelievers.

What Is The Water Jesus Was Talking About?

John 6:35

And Jesus said into them, I am the bread of life: he that cometh to me shall never hunger; and HE THAT BELIEVETH ON ME SHALL NEVER THIRSTY.

Jesus is the living water. This means that Jesus can put an end to the death ravaging the human spirit. What the Samaritan woman needed was to believe in Jesus. Faith in Jesus releases his life to be infused into us. This is what it means to be saved; his life in us prevails over the death within, causing us to be full of life in our spirit, soul and body.

Act 16:31

... Believe in the Lord Jesus Christ and thou shalt be saved, and thy house.

This woman needed to be saved! Jesus was offering her real satisfaction for her spirit, soul and body. The woman on the other hand was requesting this living water, thinking it to be a physical one.

Jesus Gives Us The True Satisfaction

John 4:15

> *The woman saith unto him, Sir, give me this water, that I thirst not, neither come hither to draw.*

A number of rich business owners, celebrities and many others popularly hailed as successful, suffer depression, with many succumbing to suicidal thoughts. With all the money they have and all the luxuries they can afford, one would think that such people would be immune to depression. Fame, money, and power may bring momentary happiness, but complete and perpetual joy comes from Jesus alone. What Jesus gives is the true satisfaction, it doesn't disappear after some time, it's always there.

1st Thessalonians 1:6

> *And ye became followers of us, and of the Lord, having received the word in much afflictions, WITH JOY OF THE HOLY GHOST.*

The joy we have as believers in Christ, is from the Holy Spirit. Our joy doesn't come from this world, it doesn't come from fame, money, or from anything else the systems of this world has to offer. Our joy comes from the Spirit of God within us, not from without. If your happiness is externally inspired, under the pressures of life you will lose it all. When a believer is faced with the pressures of life however, the joy from within ought to swallow up the pressure without. This joy is not some kind of artificial smile people often try to wear while suffering, it bubbles from within.

As children of God, there is always exceeding joy in our heart. This is because the Spirit of God within helps us see how God has subdued all our challenges through the finished work of Christ on the cross. That's why this joy is often referred to as 'the joy of the Holy Ghost'. And as you feed your heart with this kind of truth from the Holy Spirit, faith will rise in your heart to subdue every mountain you face. The water that can satisfy our spirit, soul and body comes from Jesus. Although Jesus was not referring to water literally, he said 'he that cometh to me shall never hunger; and he that believeth on me shall never thirst'.

Believing in Jesus brings us salvation; it puts an end to the death in our spirit. All the outward manifestations of death cease the moment the death on the inside has been dealt with by the life of God. This life of God flows inside out, causing us to be full of life and to experience victory at every turn. Salvation doesn't just mean to be saved from sin. The Greek word 'soteria' refers to salvation from sin, prosperity, health and deliverance. Death in the human spirit was as a result of his separation from God, there was no more relationship between us and him. Being separated from God is death and being connected to him is life. God created us to seek (desire and crave) him and this desire is in each of us. Sin ensured this need for him unattended to. He couldn't relate with us and we couldn't relate with him because of sin. Jesus came to put an end to that separation. He came to bring us into union with the father, and to bring life into our spirit through this union with God.

Ephesians 2:13

> *13 But now in Christ Jesus, ye who sometimes were far off are made nigh by the blood of Christ.*

The Lover She Never Had

John 4:16 - 19

> *16 Jesus saith unto her, Go, call thy husband, and come hither.*
> *17 The woman answered and said, I have no husband. Jesus said unto her, Thou hast well said, I have no husband:*

18 For thou hast had five husbands; and he whom thou now hast is not thy husband: in that saidst thou truly.

19 The woman saith unto him, Sir, I perceive that thou art a prophet.

From the above conversation, we can see that Jesus knew everything about the Samaritan woman yet his love for her was unchanging. How wonderful it is to know that Jesus does not relate to us according to what we have done, he relates to us according to who he is. Whatever you have done, have not done or cannot do, will not qualify or disqualify you from his love. Love is not just what he does, it's who he is. People usually want their past and mistakes covered. Jesus did not come to uncover this woman's past. He came to show her that he loved her regardless of who she was or whatever she had done. He came to show her a love not based on her merit.

At some point, this woman of Samaria would have sensed that with this man, there was no condemnation for her. Ordinarily, no religious Jew will consider coming close, even for a good Samaritan. But for this woman who had a bad reputation in the community, even her own fellow Samaritans would avoid being around her, much more a Jew. Yet, Jesus sought her out to speak with her. Jesus doesn't relate with us based on people's approval. He doesn't take permission from people to connect with us. No one can talk him out of loving us because he loved us without anyone's advice or suggestion in the first place.

People distancing themselves from the Samaritan woman for ethical or religious reasons must have reminded her of how awful she was. This would have brought her a great sense of guilt and condemnation. When people with high moral standing refuse to associate with you, and religious people have already condemned you as a sinner even without knowing you, Jesus who knows you better than they all, has his arms open wide towards you; he will never condemn you.

9
TRUE WORSHIP

John 4:20-24

20 Our fathers worshipped in this mountain; and ye say, that in Jerusalem is the place where men ought to worship.

21 Jesus saith unto her, Woman, believe me, the hour cometh, when ye shall neither in this mountain, nor yet at Jerusalem, worship the Father.

22 Ye worship ye know not what: we know what we worship: for salvation is of the Jews.

23 But the hour cometh, and now is, when the TRUE WORSHIPPERS shall worship THE FATHER in SPIRIT AND IN TRUTH: for THE FATHER SEEKETH SUCH TO WORSHIP HIM.

24 GOD IS A SPIRIT: and They THAT WORSHIP HIM MUST WORSHIP HIM IN SPIRIT AND IN TRUTH.

I n the above conversation, the Samaritan woman opens up a discussion on right or wrong worship. She was asking Jesus about what was right and who wasn't; the Samaritans worship in the mountains but the Jews worship at Jerusalem, she wanted Jesus to support or oppose this.

Jesus did not come to show us which worship is right or wrong, he came to show us what true worship is and who the true worshippers are. He didn't come to oppose or support any religion; he came to show us how to truly worship the father. From the discussion Jesus had with this woman about worship, we learn that true worshippers worship the father in spirit and in truth. Who are these people?

Philippians 3:3

For we are the circumcision, which worship God in the Spirit, and REJOICE IN CHRIST JESUS, AND HAVE NO CONFIDENCE IN THE FLESH.

The word 'rejoice' used in the above verse is 'kauchaomai' in Greek, and it means 'to glory, rejoice, boast and joy'. True worshippers boast, glory, rejoice, and joy in Christ. They don't rejoice, glory, rejoice or joy in themselves, their achievements or anything else. This kind of worship is not to replace Christ but because of him. A true worshipper boasts in Christ and not in self, in which case, both the Samaritans and the Jews were not getting it right. The last statement in Apostle Paul's writing in the verse above is a very powerful one. It says '. . . and have no confidence in the flesh'. God considers it as worship when you place your confidence in Christ not yourself. Without Jesus Christ everyone has missed it, no one can truly worship the father without Jesus.

Worship is reverence. It is worship when you esteem what Christ has done above all you can ever do. When you reverence Christ and not what you have done, it pleases God and that's what God considers true worship. There were temple sacrifices, singing Levites and a whole lot of things going on in the Jewish temple, yet Jesus said the Father was searching for worshippers. I wonder what else anyone can do to beat the thousands of sacrifices that Solomon offered, still God didn't find in Solomon a true worshipper. Has God found these true worshippers he is searching for? And if he has, who are they?

Philippians 3:3

> *FOR WE ARE THE CIRCUMCISION, WHICH WORSHIP GOD IN THE SPIRIT, and rejoice in Christ Jesus, and have no confidence in the flesh.*

A lot of people have confused a true worshipper for someone who sings songs of worship, and some think that worship has to do with cool songs and slow beats. Neither is accurate. A true worshipper glories, boasts, rejoices, and joys in Christ and not in self. Singing is one way we worship, not all of it. It is not wrong to offer service to God. Whatever we do in worship however, should not be as though what Jesus did wasn't enough, but because what he has done is more than enough. What makes a song worship to God is neither the solemn nature of the song nor that God is mentioned in it, rather a song is true worship when Christ and his finished work is exalted rather than anything we have done or can do!

The Greek word 'pietho' is what the word 'confidence' was translated from in Philippians 3:3 and it also means 'believe'. A true worshipper doesn't put his belief in anything he has done, good or bad. His belief is not in himself but in Christ.

Does this then mean that we should do nothing at all? Certainly not. A true worshipper still renders services to God in singing, giving, evangelism and preaching etc., but with an entirely different attitude.

Romans 12:1

> *I beseech you therefore, brethren, by the mercies of God, that ye present your bodies a living sacrifice, holy, acceptable unto God, which is your reasonable service.*

As true worshippers, we have the responsibility to present our bodies as a living sacrifice, that is holy and acceptable unto God, this is our reasonable service. In essence, we still have acts of service to do, but how we go about it has changed. We do all these by God's mercies, knowing that he already loves us and is pleased with us, as a result of the finished work of Jesus. Do you see that? It is because the mercies of God have come to us first that we can now present our bodies as a living sacrifice.

Romans 12:1 (NIV)

> *Therefore, I urge you, brothers and sisters, IN VIEW OF GOD'S MERCY, to offer your bodies as a living sacrifice, holy and pleasing to God—this is your true and proper worship.*

We don't need to do anything to get God to be pleased with us because he is already pleased. In view of his mercy upon us through what Christ has done, we present our bodies a living sacrifice, holy, acceptable unto God, which is our reasonable service. According to the New International Version, this is our true and proper worship.

Romans 12:1 (TPT)

> *Beloved friends, what should be OUR PROPER RESPONSE TO GOD'S MARVELOUS MERCIES? I encourage you to SURRENDER YOURSELVES*

TO GOD TO BE HIS SACRED, LIVING SACRIFICES. AND LIVE IN HOLINESS, experiencing all that delights his heart. FOR THIS BECOMES YOUR GENUINE EXPRESSION OF WORSHIP.

The focus is on Jesus and not yourself. It is reverence to focus on Jesus rather than yourself. His mercy causes us to surrender to him. So, we are responding to God's mercies and not trying to make ourselves try to achieve it by our works. The Passion Translation puts it beautifully, '. . . For this becomes your genuine expression of worship'. Wow! That's amazing! You will notice that The Passion Translation used the word 'worship' instead of the word 'service' as used in the King James Version. This is correct because the Greek word 'latreia' translated as 'service' in the King James Version also means worship.

Isaiah 12:1

And in that day thou shalt say, O Lord, I will praise thee: though thou wast angry with me, thine anger is turned away, and thou comfortedst me.

In this passage Isaiah describes a day when we will say 'O Lord, I will praise thee'. Why are we praising and what is the reason for the praise? It's because 'though thou wast angry with me, thine anger is turned away, and thou comfortedst me'. The praise or adoration given to God in this verse is not to appease him but because he is at peace with us.

This day being talked about here is not just a certain day in the human calendar like Monday, Tuesday, Wednesday and so on. Isaiah was referring to a dispensation, the day when God's anger will be turned away from us, which is the time we are now living in. If this was about a specific date, then only those alive on the day Jesus was crucified and God's anger was turned should be the ones to praise, yet this is not so.

The reason for our praise is because God's anger has been turned away from everyone, including those who were not physically present on the day Jesus died. Since we were included in the salvation plan, we are also among those who will respond in praise to God. We are the people who are to respond with adoration to him because of his grace to us. This is who we are. Paul rightly said that we are the circumcision who worship the father in spirit and in truth. We are true worshippers because we responded by faith in the finished work of Christ and not what we have done. His great act of salvation always comes first and evokes our response of reverence to him. True worship is in response to what Christ has done. A true worshipper is one who puts faith in what Christ has done above what he could ever do by himself, in order to earn a relationship with God. A true worshipper approaches the Father by faith, not by works of self-righteousness.

Isaiah 12: 2

> *Behold, God is my salvation; I will trust, and not be afraid: for the Lord Jehovah is my strength and my song; he also is become my salvation.*

What he has done for us is our strength and confidence. He is not just the person we sing for or sing to, he is our song. This means that without what he has done, we are weak and there is nothing to sing about. Any song, message, evangelism, prayer, fasting, offering, service that doesn't reflect what Christ has done as more than enough for bringing us salvation, is not worship.

Romans 12:1 (MSG)

> *So here's what I want you to do, God helping you: Take your*

everyday, ordinary life—your sleeping, eating, going-to-work, and walking-around life—and place it before God as an offering. EMBRACING WHAT GOD DOES FOR YOU IS THE BEST THING YOU CAN DO FOR HIM.

Our Lord Jesus did a complete work on Calvary, thus God is already pleased with us. Solomon offered thousands of animals to God and built a magnificent temple for God. David wrote many songs and even made a large donation for the building of the temple. Moses and Elijah fasted forty days, the three Hebrew boys faced fire because of their faith in God, Daniel faced the lions because of his faith too, yet against the background of these great acts, Jesus said God was seeking true worshippers. This means that God did not find any true worshipper throughout human history prior to Jesus' arrival. Otherwise God would have instructed all others to follow that person's pattern of worship in order to also be called true worshippers. In Philippians 3:3, the Holy Spirit speaking through Apostle Paul said we are those who worship in spirit and in truth. In us God found what he wanted; a people who magnify what he has done by looking away from what we have done, a people not seeking to do anything more to earn anything from him. Let's examine one of the conversations Jesus had with the Jews on a similar issue.

John 6:28

> *Then said they unto him, WHAT SHALL WE DO, THAT WE MIGHT WORK THE WORKS OF GOD?*

What does God want you to do to please him? Even the Jews in Jesus' days wanted to know what to do in order to truly please God. They must have expected to hear a list of dos and don'ts, but what Jesus presented seemed too easy to be true.

John 6:29

Jesus answered and said unto them, THIS IS THE WORK OF GOD, THAT YE BELIEVE ON HIM WHOM HE HATH SENT.

Many times, seemingly easy things turn out to be the most difficult to do. For instance, it is harder to simply rest and believe that you are pleasing God, than to get that confidence from observing a list of rules. It makes sense to believe you are doing what God wants when you observe some rules. To accept that you only have to believe in Jesus and that believing pleases God more than anything you can ever do, is no easy feat for those who prefer to trust in what they can do and see. God places faith over any human works. Faith pleases God because it magnifies him. The law magnifies what we can do, and these works of self righteousness are as filthy rags before him. Faith agrees that Christ has done it all and that what he did is more than enough.

Hebrews 11:6

But without faith it is impossible to please him...

True worship is faith in the person of Jesus. Nobody can worship God without Jesus. If there was anything we could do to please the father as worship, Jesus would not have come. Jesus has done everything the law required of us that we couldn't do. Anything we do henceforth should be in response to what Christ has done.

Our singing, giving, dancing, evangelism and everything else should be in response to God's love towards us. This is true worship, because it reveres Christ and not our performance. In this way, we honour what Christ has done and not what we do.

Because God is pleased with us doesn't mean we should begin to lead reckless lives. Romans 12 says that it's reasonable for us to revere God now because he is already pleased with us. In the same breath, it will be unreasonable for us to now start trusting ourselves to do something to please or displease a God who is already pleased with us. The Bible says that without faith it is impossible to please God. Impossible simply means impossible. No fasting will do, no sacrifice will do, nothing pleases God than faith. It's faith to believe that God sees you as a true worshipper even when you have not lifted a hand in worship. It's faith to believe that Christ, with nail-pierced arms stretched out, took all the judgement you deserved.

Many times people want to do something so they can brag about how good they are. They want to show how hard they've worked. Religious people want God to give them laws, a list of do's and don'ts, so they can compare themselves to others in self-righteousness. The Bible clearly shows that the law is good but the man who received the law was a sinner by nature. As such, the law was not given so that mankind can be justified by keeping it, but to show us how impossible it is for us to keep God's laws.

Galatians 3:19

> *WHEREFORE THEN SERVETH THE LAW? IT WAS ADDED BECAUSE OF TRANSGRESSIONS, till the seed should come to whom the promise was made; and it was ordained by angels in the hand of a mediator.*

The law was given because of transgressions. Transgression means sin. The law was given because man was a sinner and needed a saviour to deliver him. The verse above explains that the law was given so that man will come to the end of himself; his inability to fully keep the law would make him realise that he is a helpless sinner who cannot save himself by anything he can do. He would thus stop trying to earn salvation by his efforts and instead come to see his need of a saviour. The law shows man how totally helpless he is and how desperately he needs a saviour.

Psalm 130: 3-4

> *3 If thou, LORD, shouldest mark iniquities, O Lord, who shall stand? 4 But THERE IS FORGIVENESS WITH THEE, THAT THOU MAYEST BE FEARED.*

The word 'feared' in Hebrew is also translated as 'reverence'. When Jesus spoke about true worship, the word 'worship' also meant 'to do reverence' in the Greek. Another translation puts it this way;

Psalm 130: 4 (New Heart English Bible)

> *But there is forgiveness with you, so that you may be revered.*

True worship or reverence is a result of God's love towards us; because he has given us the forgiveness of sin we don't deserve instead of the judgement we deserve. Our worship is not to get anything from him but rather it's a response to what he has already done. His forgiveness comes before our worship or reverence. True worship is to honour what Christ has done above our efforts. True worship is to believe in his grace rather than your efforts. It is to reverence him because of his love and kindness towards you. Jesus said that we do what God wants us to do by believing in the Son.

John 6:29

> *Jesus answered and said unto them, THIS IS THE WORK OF GOD, THAT YE BELIEVE ON HIM WHOM HE HATH SENT.*

At this point, I will try to use another story to further unpack the topic of our discussion and make it clearer. It is the story of the woman with the alabaster box.

Luke 7:37-50

> *37 And, behold, a woman in the city, which was a sinner, when she knew that Jesus sat at meat in the Pharisee's house, brought an alabaster box of ointment,*
>
> *38 AND STOOD AT HIS FEET BEHIND HIM WEEPING, AND BEGAN TO WASH HIS FEET WITH TEARS, AND DID WIPE THEM WITH THE HAIRS OF HER HEAD, AND KISSED HIS FEET, AND ANOINTED THEM WITH THE OINTMENT.*
>
> *39 Now when the Pharisee which had bidden him saw it, he spake within himself, saying, THIS MAN, IF HE WERE A PROPHET, WOULD HAVE KNOWN WHO AND WHAT MANNER OF WOMAN THIS IS THAT TOUCHETH HIM: FOR SHE IS A SINNER.*
>
> *40 And Jesus answering said unto him, Simon, I have somewhat to say unto thee. And he saith, Master, say on.*
>
> *41 There was a certain creditor which had two debtors: the one owed five hundred pence, and the other fifty.*
>
> *42 And when they had nothing to pay, he frankly forgave them both. Tell me therefore, which of them will love him most?*
>
> *43 Simon answered and said, I suppose that he, to whom he forgave most. And he said unto him, Thou hast rightly judged.*
>
> *44 And he turned to the woman, and said unto Simon, Seest thou this woman? I entered into thine house, thou gavest me no water for my feet: but she hath washed my feet with tears, and wiped them with the hairs of her head.*

45 THOU GAVEST ME NO KISS: BUT THIS WOMAN SINCE THE TIME I CAME IN HATH NOT CEASED TO KISS MY FEET.

46 My head with oil thou didst not anoint: but this woman hath anointed my feet with ointment.

47 Wherefore I say unto thee, Her sins, which are many, are forgiven; for she loved much: but TO WHOM LITTLE IS FORGIVEN, THE SAME LOVETH LITTLE.

48 And he said unto her, Thy sins are forgiven.

49 And they that sat at meat with him began to say within themselves, WHO IS THIS THAT FORGIVETH SINS ALSO?

50 AND HE SAID TO THE WOMAN, THY FAITH HATH SAVED THEE; GO IN PEACE.

What an interesting story we have here. This woman went right behind Jesus, she didn't go in front. She knew how undeserving she was to come face to face with the Saviour, she knew she couldn't have earned it. So she went behind him, putting her trust in his goodness and not in anything she had done. It is clear that her aim from the onset was to give all her best to him, so down she went, washed his feet with her tears and wiped them with her hair.

This is a big wonder. No woman does this kind of thing to her hair. Every woman treats her hair very specially. Some men cannot even dare touch their wife's hair without her consent. For this woman though, the hair she cherished so much went down on the feet of Jesus. Even her perfume, worth a full year wage of a worker at the time, was poured upon Jesus. Mark's gospel says that the perfume was worth more than three hundred pence. In the book of Matthew, it was recorded that a labourer's wage was about a penny a day, implying that this woman gave an equivalent of one year labourer's wage.

Matthew 20: 1-2

> *1 For the Kingdom of heaven is like unto a man that is an householder, which went out early in the morning to hire labourers into his vineyard.*
>
> *2 And WHEN HE HAD AGREED WITH THE LABOURERS FOR A PENNY A DAY, he sent them into his vineyard.*

I have never in my life seen a woman with this kind of gesture towards her husband, so for a person like Jesus who wasn't even married to this woman to receive such, shows how much reverence and honour she had for Jesus. A man once humorously told his wife, 'if the way you smile each time you see your siblings is the same way you smile when you see me, we wouldn't have any troubles at all'. Every married man I know wants a wife who will be submissive to him but hardly knows what stirs submission without force. From Jesus, we learn that unconditional love makes reverence or respect possible and achievable.

Luke 7: 47-48

> *47 Wherefore I say unto thee, Her sins, which are many, are forgiven; for she loved much: but TO WHOM LITTLE IS FORGIVEN, THE SAME LOVETH LITTLE.*
>
> *48 And he said unto her, Thy sins are forgiven.*

Just in case you were asking, why did this woman love this much? The answer is clearly written here '...to whom little is forgiven, the same loveth little'. She was forgiven much! A person who is forgiven little loves little, but a person forgiven much loves much!

The word translated as 'worship' is the word 'proskuneo' which means to kiss, prostrate, reverence and worship. This implies that when this woman was kissing the feet of Jesus, she was actually showing her reverence (worship) for him. Some bible scholars opine that this woman was the same one caught in adultery who was to be stoned to death but was saved by Jesus from those who wanted to kill her.

Perhaps this is so or not, but what I have tried to do by including her story here, is to show you that true worship is a response to God's grace towards us. Worship is because of salvation; our worship to God is a consequence of his unconditional love towards us. We are awed by his goodness towards us and this causes us to respond in reverence towards him. When we were undeserving Jesus died for us, the knowledge of his love is what propels true worship.

True Worship Is To The Father

It is impossible to worship a God you do not know. Jesus told the Samaritan woman about God and this time he introduced him as 'the Father'.

John 4:23

But the hour cometh, and now is, when the true worshippers shall worship THE FATHER in spirit and in truth: for the father seeketh such to worship him.

Many people claim to know God but they actually have no clue about him. Because you have been in the Church for many years does not automatically mean you have a true revelation of who God is. Being born into a Christian family does not mean you have a correct knowledge of God either, nor does religious titles and denominational affiliations equate having a true revelation of who God is.

Jesus uses the word 'the Father' and not 'a Father'. He wasn't talking about another God nor was he talking about another Father. He was specifically referring to one person 'the Father'. Jesus did not come to give us rules and regulations to keep, he came to reveal the father to us. The Samaritan woman had never known God as Father. She never thought a holy God would ever want anything to do with her. Now, for the first time in her life, she was hearing that God was not just some being far away in the sky, she was hearing that he was not just God, he was 'Father'. That word connoted someone who had a special love for her.

Our Father in heaven does not want you to see him as just a spirit being out there in the sky, whom people call 'God', he wants to be a Father to you. Your father in heaven wants to have a personal relationship with you. He wants you to worship or reverence him as his child and not as his subject. The kind of relationship he wants with you is such that you can look up to him and say 'Daddy', not a relationship where it seems you are walking on eggshells around him all the time. The kind of relationship he wants with you is one based on his love for you.

10

WHO IS THE FATHER?

John 14:8-9

8 Philip saith unto him, Lord, shew us the Father, and it sufficeth us.

9 Jesus saith unto him, have I been so long time with you, and yet hast thou not known me, Philip? He that hath seen me hath seen the Father; and how sayest thou then, Shew us the Father?

Colossians 1:15

Who is the IMAGE OF THE INVISIBLE GOD, the firstborn of every creature:

Logically speaking, invisible things do not have an image, only visible things can. Spiritually however, Jesus is the image of the Father revealed. The father who is invisible becomes visible and clearly seen in Jesus. In Jesus, the nature and character of our heavenly father is clearly observable, the invisible made visible to us.

Before Jesus came no man had seen God, but once he arrived on earth, the invisible God was revealed to us. Sometimes I love to say it this way, "God was saying 'this is me' when Jesus was born on the Earth". You may never have had a supernatural vision of God, yet when you see God revealed in the person of Jesus through the bible, your experience is not inferior to those who have seen him in any other way apart from the word. Jesus said to Thomas 'blessed are those who have not seen yet believe'.

We may not have seen Jesus physically but through the bible we see him, we know him, and we are able to tell of his true nature. We know our Father is full of grace because Jesus is full of grace. We know the Father loves us because this was demonstrated to us by the sacrifice of Jesus. We are no longer afraid to call him Daddy, the true knowledge of him has wiped out every fear. No fear can lurk around our hearts in the darkest night or on the brightest day. He is our Daddy; he is on our side no matter what happens. Even when we fail, he remains faithful to us. He doesn't relate to us based on what we've done but based on what Christ has done.

Some people imagine God to be an angry old man up in the cloud who cannot wait to smack them with blistering thunder when they sin. They think God is a taskmaster whose unending demands have to be kept else it rains fire, hail and brimstone.

1 John 5:20

> *And we know that THE SON OF GOD IS COME, AND HATH GIVEN US AN UNDERSTANDING, THAT WE MAY KNOW HIM THAT IS TRUE, and we are in him that is true, even in his Son Jesus Christ. This is the true God, and eternal life.*

The word 'know' as used above is from the Greek word 'ginosko', a Jewish idiom for intercourse. This implies intimacy. Jesus came to reveal the father to us. In Christ, we come to know God intimately and personally. It is only in Jesus that we see God as our loving, just, righteous and merciful Daddy. Jesus came to bring us into union with the Father. He came to reveal the Father to us. In Jesus we clearly see who God really is, his true nature and character.

See Who The Father Truly Is

Micah 7:18

> *Who is a God like unto thee, that pardoneth iniquity and passeth by the transgression of the remnant of his heritage? He retaineth not his anger for ever, because he delighteth in mercy.*

From the above verse, one thing is obvious; showing mercy is God's hobby! His willingness to show mercy surpasses your ability to sin. He delights and takes pleasure in showing mercy.

Jeremiah 9: 24

> *24 But let him that glorieth glory in this, that he understandeth and knoweth me, that I am the LORD which exercise loving-kindness, judgement, and righteousness, in the Earth: for in these things I delight, saith the LORD.*

What does it mean when God says he delights in loving-kindness, judgement, and righteousness? If that's a question on your mind, I will show you another scripture that explains this further.

Hosea 2: 19

> *And I will betroth thee unto me for ever; yea, I will betroth thee unto me in righteousness, and in judgement, and in lovingkindness, and in mercies.*

By his loving-kindness, judgement, and righteousness, God brings us into union with him. He is a God who delights in these because by it he betroths us to himself. God is delighted because by these he won us to be his own. God betroths us to himself by righteousness, judgement and loving-kindness. If this is not the God you know then something is wrong. This God does not make you his own because of your good sense, moral judgement, righteousness or any lovingkindness you have towards him. These things are good but they cannot bring you into union with God, neither can they earn you anything from him. We come into union with God by his own goodness and not ours. It's by his grace from start to finish. Let's take a further study into the bible to see what it has to say about our Father being a God who delights in loving-kindness, judgement, righteousness and mercy.

a. His Lovingkindness

In his loving-kindness God sent his son to die for our sins.

John 3:16.
> *For God so loved the world, that he gave his only begotten Son, that whosoever believeth in him should not perish, but have everlasting life.*

God's love towards us is unconditional; there's nothing we did to deserve it and there's nothing we have done that can disqualify us from it. By his great love Jesus made us his bride. He betrothed us to himself and brought us into union with him.

1st John 4:9
> *In this was manifested the love of God towards us, because that God sent his only begotten Son into the world, that we might live through him.*

b. His Judgement

In his judgement God did not let sin go unpunished, nor did he allow the sinner to die for his sin. He placed the judgement for our sin on Jesus and this satisfied his wrath. He is not a God who delights in injustice. He hates sin and won't let sin go unpunished. It's in Christ we see how God delights in judgement. When man was trapped by his sin and deserved judgement, God did not, because of his loving-kindness, let the sin go unpunished. In the same breath, he did not allow man to bear the judgement for sin because carrying the death sentence by himself would mean eternal damnation for man. Instead, it pleased God to place all the punishment for our sin on Jesus. This showed how much God hates sin and how unwilling he is to let it go unpunished. By this great judgement passed on Jesus on the cross, we are saved.

Isaiah 53: 10 -11

> *10 Yet IT PLEASED THE LORD TO BRUISE HIM; he hath put him to grief: when thou shalt make his soul an offering for sin, he shall see his seed, he shall prolong his days, and the pleasure of the LORD shall prosper in his hand.*
>
> *11 He shall see of the travail of his soul, and shall be satisfied: by his knowledge shall my righteous servant justify many; for he shall bear their iniquities.*

On the basis of the death of Jesus on the cross, God's judgement has been satisfied. He took our death sentence and as a result of this, we are justified from all sins. All our sins are forgiven.

2nd Corinthians 5:14

> *For the love of Christ constraineth us; because we thus judge that IF ONE DIED FOR ALL, THEN WERE ALL DEAD:*

Anyone who rejects this truth will have to face God's judgement by himself. Our God doesn't delight in sin, neither does he delight to see the ones he loves perish. In Christ Jesus, God's judgement and justice system is clearly seen.

c. His Righteousness

By his righteousness we are made righteous. We receive the righteousness of Christ through his death on the cross. He took our sin and gave us his righteousness! We don't do anything to be righteous, we are righteous by putting our faith in the finished work of Jesus. Righteousness does not mean right doing, it means to have right standing with God, to stand before God without any feeling of guilt, shame and condemnation.

Romans 5: 17

> *17 For if by one man's offence death reigned by one; much more they which receive abundance of grace and of the gift of righteousness shall reign in life by one, Jesus Christ.*

By one - Jesus Christ, we received the free gift of righteousness. Under the Old Testament, you needed to fulfil the law to become righteous or to have right standing with God, but in this New Covenant, our righteousness is a gift, based on what Christ has done. The Father counts us righteous when we put our faith in Jesus. This is who the father is.

Romans 4:5

> *But to him that worketh not, but believeth on him that justifieth the ungodly, his faith is counted for righteousness.*

'Righteousness is the nature of God which when imparted to the human spirit produces the rightness of God' - Pst. Chris Oyakilome

This means we receive a new nature of righteousness when we put our faith in Jesus. As such, the nature of Adam (the sin nature) is no longer in us. It's possible to do God's will now because we have the nature of God; the tendencies and proclivities to do good deeds are now within us. Consequently, we are not doing good deeds to be good but because we are now by nature, good. God's righteousness within us makes it easier for us to live right unconsciously than we can ever do deliberately with the nature of sin.

Our Heavenly Father has brought us into right standing with him by his grace. He has gifted us the right to be called righteous. By the sacrifice of Jesus, he took our sins and offered us his righteousness. When we believe in him by putting our faith in what he has done, we receive his righteousness as a gift, not as a reward based on our own good works.

Romans 5:17

> *17 For if by one man's offence death reigned by one; much more they which RECEIVE ABUNDANCE OF GRACE AND OF THE GIFT OF RIGHTEOUSNESS shall reign in life by one, Jesus Christ.*

Through our Father's love, righteousness is received as a gift, not earned. There is nothing you do to get a gift otherwise whatever you receive is no longer a gift but a reward. The biggest alert to ever hit a bank is the righteousness God credits to you when you believe in the finished work of Christ. This is who the Father is! He doesn't want us to go about trying to earn our righteousness before we can come to him. By the sacrifice of Jesus he has earned us our right to be called righteous. We receive this righteousness when we put our faith in Jesus. The first time the word 'righteousness' was used in the bible was in reference to Abraham. God declared him righteous because of his faith and not his good works.

Genesis 15:6

> *And he believed God in the Lord; and he counted it to him for righteousness.*

In the New Testament, Paul referred back to this statement and made clearer to us what had transpired at the time.

Gal 3:6-8

> *6 Even as Abraham believed God, and it was accounted to him for righteousness.*
>
> *7 Know ye therefore that they which are of faith, the same are the children of Abraham.*
>
> *8 AND THE SCRIPTURE, FORESEEING THAT GOD WOULD JUSTIFY THE HEATHEN THROUGH FAITH, PREACHED BEFORE THE GOSPEL UNTO ABRAHAM, saying, in thee shall all nations be blessed.*

God revealed the gospel (good news) of his great plan to redeem mankind to himself, to Abraham. Abraham became righteous simply because he believed it and not because of anything else he did.

d. His Mercy

None of these good things our Father has done for us are based on our performance but on his mercy towards us. In his mercy he joined us to himself. Eternity took on time; the son of God became the son of man, and by this he redeemed us to himself. This is the kind of Father he is.

When people are betrothed in the Jewish culture they are considered legally married. Since we are betrothed to him, we share in everything he has. His love has become our love; we are able to love like him because his love abides in us. His judgement is our judgement; since he has been judged, we have been judged, when he died our death sentence was served. His righteousness is our righteousness and by his mercy we have obtained mercy.

Titus 3:4-5

> *4 But after that the kindness and love of God our Saviour toward man appeared,*
>
> *5 Not by works of righteousness which we have done, but ACCORDING TO HIS MERCY HE SAVED US, by the washing of regeneration, and renewing of the Holy Ghost;*

Ephesians 2:4-5

> *4 But GOD, WHO IS RICH IN MERCY, for his great love wherewith he loved us,*
>
> *5 Even when we were dead in sins, hath quickened us together with Christ, (by grace ye are saved;)*

We have been made to share with him equally in everything he has. If he loves then we can love. If he has been judged, we have been judged. If he is righteous then we are righteous, and if he is merciful, we can be merciful because of his mercy towards us. As God has become our Father, whatever he has, has become ours by inheritance because we are part of his family. We have his life, his power and his nature in us. God delights when we know him this way. It pleases him when we know him as a God of loving-kindness rather than as one who takes pleasure in the death of a sinner.

His Love Destroys The Power Of Sin

When we know God as our Father, it becomes possible to reverence him. It becomes possible for us to cast our full weight on him without any fear that he will let us fall. We will love him and desire to please him in response to understanding his fatherhood. Knowing God intimately will make faith rise in our hearts. Through this kind of relationship, we will be able to believe that he loves us enough to give us whatever we desire. The easiest way to live free from sin is to receive the father's love.

1st John 2:15

> *Love not the world, neither the things that are in the world. IF ANY MAN LOVE THE WORLD, THE LOVE OF THE FATHER IS NOT IN HIM.*

When you know and believe that God loves you, you will not want to sin. 'Well I know so and so who is a believer, yet he is still living in sin' some people may wonder. Going to church won't make you a believer, any more than going to a forest will make you a tree. If you know and believe that the name your parents call you is your real name, when you are out on the street and hear a random name, you wouldn't respond would you? True knowledge affects action. If whatever you claim to know doesn't affect your actions then you don't truly know it. The bible says if any man loves the world he doesn't have the father's love in him; he hasn't received the love of the Father.

His Love Causes Rejoicing

Philippians 3:3

> *For we are the circumcision, which worship God in the Spirit, and REJOICE IN CHRIST JESUS, AND HAVE NO CONFIDENCE IN THE FLESH.*

When you truly and correctly know the Father, and have put your trust in his great love towards you, you will have a positive attitude of joy. When we know God as our Father and rest our faith in his love, without putting any confidence on who we are or what we have done, that knowledge will cause us to be full of rejoicing. Our hearts will know no limit to joy. Remember we've established that the word 'rejoice' as used in the above is 'kauchaomai' in the Greek, and it means to glory, rejoice, boast and joy.

A true worshipper who knows that God is his Father, or better put, 'Daddy', will be confident. Without any encouragement or external prodding, such ones will naturally begin to boast, glory, rejoice, and joy in Christ alone. They will not boast, glory, rejoice or joy in themselves or their achievements, their faith in the Father's love will cause them to be full of joy. It's impossible to be depressed when you know the extent of the Father's love for you, because you will always be full of joy and won't have space for worries, anxieties and fear. So if you ever find yourself feeling overwhelmed by any negative emotions, start focusing on the Father's love for you. Jesus is the picture of who our heavenly father is. If the Jesus you know doesn't look like the one described above, then you have met the wrong Jesus. Jesus is the embodiment of God's love; he did not come to condemn the sinner but to condemn sin.

John 3:17

> *For God sent not his Son into the world to condemn the world; but that the world through him might be saved.*

Our Father doesn't condemn the sinner; he hates sin but he loves the sinner. This is the reason why he sent Jesus; to show how much he hates sin by punishing Jesus, and in the same vein show how much he loves you - the sinner, by not letting you face your death sentence by yourself.

11
THE POWER OF GOD'S LOVE

John 4:25 -26

25 The woman saith unto him, I know that MESSIAS cometh, which is called Christ: when he is come, he will tell us all things.
26 JESUS SAITH UNTO HER, I THAT SPEAK UNTO THEE AM HE.

Our Saviour did a complete work, it covered all our sins and its consequences, nothing was left untouched. The blood of Jesus atoned for all the sins of the world. We all have been made free because of this great salvation brought to us through Jesus.

All Sins Have Been Forgiven

Psalms 103: 1-3 (NIV)

1 Praise the LORD, my soul, and all that is within me, praise his holy name.

2 Praise the LORD, my soul, and do not forget all his benefits;

3 WHO FORGIVES ALL YOUR SINS; who heals all your diseases;

Col 2:13 (ESV)

13 You were dead through your trespasses and the uncircumcision of your flesh. He made you alive together with him, HAVING FORGIVEN US ALL OUR TRESPASSES

Heb 10:12

But this man, after he had OFFERED ONE SACRIFICE for sins for ever, SAT DOWN on the right hand of God;

Every sin has been forgiven. If it were only our past sins then the bible would not have said 'all'. There is no sin that the blood of Jesus did not cleanse us from. All our sins - past, present and future, have been forgiven. Jesus sat down in heaven only because the work was completed. In the Old Testament the High Priest does not sit down. When he is done making atonement for sin he leaves the temple, to return the next year and every other year, in order to continually offer the sin offering for his people. But Jesus our Saviour accomplished this with one sacrifice, after which he sat down. He sat because the work is finished.

Isaiah 38: 17 - 18 (NKJV)

Behold for peace I had great bitterness: but THOU HAST IN LOVE TO MY SOUL delivered it from the pit of corruption: for thou hast CAST ALL MY SINS BEHIND THY BACK.

When God judged Christ on our behalf, he placed all our sin behind himself. This means that God has removed all our sins out of his sight. If God doesn't see it any more, stop hunting for it. Don't let the devil, anyone or anything trick you into believing that God is angry with you because of any sin you have committed, when the word of God says you have been forgiven. In case you are wondering how this kind of forgiveness came to be, see another scripture;

Heb 9:22

> *And almost all things are by the law purged with blood; and WITHOUT SHEDDING OF BLOOD IS NO REMISSION.*

When Jesus shed his blood on the cross due to God's judgement on him, all our sins were forgiven. The acceptance of Jesus' sacrifice meant that God's judgement had been served and on that ground, we have been forgiven. This assurance is not only when you are good. If you ever miss it again, Jesus will not need to come back and die afresh. His blood is greater than all your sins and that blood has got you covered. Even now, He stands before God as proof that your sins have been judged.

1st John 2:1-2

> *1 My little children, these things write I unto you, that ye sin not. And if any man sin, we have an advocate with the Father, Jesus Christ the righteous:*
> *2 And he is the propitiation for our sins: and not for ours only, but also FOR THE SINS OF THE WHOLE WORLD.*

The fear of some people is that this kind of message will make believers wallow in sin, in reality, not at all. The good news of God's love doesn't make people sin but rather makes them live righteously as they ought to. By faith in what Christ has done for us, we are able to overcome sin effortlessly. If we choose to deal with sin using our self effort or willpower, we will end up struggling. Self-help is the reason many people, even believers, only enjoy periodic success over sin or addictions.

'...She Left Her Waterpot, And Went Her Way...'

John 4:27-28

27 And upon this came his disciples, and marvelled that he talked with the woman: yet no man said, What seekest thou? or, Why talkest thou with her?

28 The woman then left her water-pot, and went her way into the city, and saith to the men,

You don't need to leave anything to meet Jesus, when you meet him you will leave everything keeping you bound in a place of defeat. Many times people think they need to do something before they can come to Jesus. They try to make resolutions and endless promises to change their behaviour. Once you think there is something you can do to be pure from sin by yourself, you have started heading towards failure. If your trust is in self effort for righteousness, then the grace of God is rendered useless in your life. To experience God's grace, you need to completely rest on Christ and his finished work.

God doesn't need you to leave anything, he knows you cannot help yourself. God knows about that weight of sin that has held you bound, and he cares. He knows that the Well and the Waterpot cannot satisfy you. He knows you have become tied up with a system that doesn't work. He knows that you hurt, and he is not going to lay any burden on you, rather he wants you to unload all your burdens on him. If you are struggling with any sin, it's because you have not received his love or maybe you have lost consciousness of it. The moment your eyes are not on his love, your hands will be on the waterpot. Once your eyes behold his love, you will let go of the waterpot.

The well may look big compared to the waterpot, still both are nothing to be compared with the capacity and size of our saviour, Jesus! The waterpot is figurative. It's an entanglement of sorts, representing the things that take your eyes of Jesus and make you put your trust in self, man or other such things, for the satisfaction of your soul. You cannot break out of any entanglement by your strength. It is the knowledge of his love that empowers you to live free from sin; it destroys the power of sin over you. Some people believe what they need is therapy; there are also those who think that all they need is counselling. Please don't get me wrong, therapy and counselling is good. They both have their place and can help us in a lot of ways, but they cannot deal with the sin nature.

Without Jesus telling the woman what to do, or giving her a list of dos and don'ts, she left her waterpot willingly. She didn't leave her waterpot when she discovered he was a nice Jew. Even when she noticed that Jesus could tell her things about her that were impossible for an ordinary human to know, she didn't drop the pot. In the end, it was not his theological prowess or the accuracy of exegesis that got this woman to drop her pot, but the revelation of Jesus as her messiah. In essence, all our messages and bible studies are useful only if they point the listeners to Jesus as the messiah. Immediately she heard 'I that speak unto you, I'm he', she left her waterpot.

John 4:25-28

> *25 The woman saith unto him, I know that Messias cometh, which is called Christ: when he is come, he will tell us all things.*
> *26 Jesus saith unto her, I that speak unto thee am he*

27 And upon this came his disciples, and marvelled that he talked with the woman: yet no man said, What seekest thou? or, Why talkest thou with her?

28 The woman then left her water-pot, and went her way into the city...

The point is not that our niceness, spiritual gifts and depth of scripture are not useful. However, they are useful as a means, not as an end. If our interactions with the lost end as a nice entertaining time without pointing to Jesus, the goal has been defeated. My prayer is that our gifting, wealth of knowledge and virtues will be used by God to reveal himself. I pray that we will learn how to release ourselves to be used by God to reach the lost and not keep trying to reach the lost without him. When people get to know Jesus as the messiah, they will leave their waterpots. The reason is simple; a change has happened inside.

Romans 5:12

Wherefore, as by one man sin entered into the world, and death by sin; and so death passed upon all men, for that all have sinned:

Anyone who is born into this world has been condemned to eternal death. Since this problem came about by birth, God used rebirth (being born again) to correct the defect. As such, anyone trying to tame the sin action by self effort will not succeed, the problem is deeper than what a set dos and don'ts can solve. Laws may modify the outward behaviour for a while and to some extent, yet the proclivity to sin remains inside untouched. Until the inner instinct changes nothing else changes. Unless a sinner is changed from inside, nothing truly changes. The law is powerless to change anyone because it cannot alter a person's nature inwardly, only the messiah can save people from their sin.

Romans 8:3

> *For what the law could not do, in that it was weak through the flesh, God sending his own Son in the likeness of sinful flesh, and for sin, condemned sin in the flesh:*

What the law could not do, Jesus has done for us. Therefore, there is nothing you need to do as a form of reverence than to believe that it is done.

When You Encounter The Love Of God You Can't Keep Silent

The next thing the Samaritan woman did was to go back into the city and share the good news about the messiah (the one who saves), without anyone instructing her to. Prior to now, we had seen Jesus send out his disciples two by two, this time however, we see just one woman going out on a mission after her first meeting with the messiah. This Samaritan woman brought out her city to Jesus without any theological expertise, simply with the knowledge and her personal experience of God's love.

John 4:28-29

> *28 The woman then left her water-pot, and WENT HER WAY INTO THE CITY, AND SAITH TO THE MEN,*
> *29 COME, SEE A MAN, which told me all things that ever I did: IS NOT THIS THE CHRIST?*

All of a sudden, a woman who used to pull men to herself was now pulling them to Jesus. This time she wasn't using her feminine charm but the good news about the messiah, the saviour of the world. She who, once upon a time, could not let go of men, could now lead them to Jesus. She had been dealing with men on a one by one basis, but now she was pulling out a city.

John 4:30

Then they went out of the city, and came unto him.

Many times we think we need to pray and fast in order to save souls. Others may imagine that a Bible School certification is what is needed to be an effective soul winner. Without doubt, all these are important, yet nothing beats the power of this good news of God's unconditional love. It doesn't matter how much effort we put in, without this good news, we will be frustrated.

A good Bible School or Evangelism Training Class is one that imparts you with the knowledge of God's unconditional love for all mankind, anything away from this is useless. You may not meet Jesus in a spectacular way like the Samaritan woman did, but God's written word shows us how much he loves us by the sacrifice of Jesus. Anyone who believes in the written word will have the same experience as those who saw Jesus in person.

John 4:39-42

39 And many of the Samaritans of that city believed on him for the saying of the woman, which testified, He told me all that ever I did.

40 So when the Samaritans were come unto him, they besought him that he would tarry with them: and he abode there two days.

41 AND MANY MORE BELIEVED BECAUSE OF HIS OWN WORD;

42 And said unto the woman, now we believe, not because of thy saying: for we have heard him ourselves, and know that this is indeed the Christ, the Saviour of the world.

As we proclaim the goodness of God everywhere, many will believe. This good news will cause men to receive a new life. No one can be saved without hearing the gospel. The responsibility to share this gospel is on us. The more we know his love, the easier it is for us to speak about it and take our cities for Jesus. When you get to know how much God loves you, you will win more souls effortlessly than you have done with all your efforts, what to say will not be an issue. Reaching out will not be something you do only on evangelism day, it will become a lifestyle.

The Samaritan woman found real satisfaction, but not from man. This time her satisfaction came from a personal relationship with the Father. Nothing satisfies man's Spirit, Soul and Body than a personal relationship with our heavenly Father. This can only be achieved through faith in the Messiah (Jesus). When the woman of Samaria came in contact with God's love, she immediately took a city on her first try. Perhaps too much knowledge has become our problem. We seem to know every formula except for the one thing that matters; faith in the love of our Father. The base for every great exploit in soul winning is the knowledge of God's love. The love of God is what changes us from inside out. All the struggles of this lady ended the moment she came in contact with the Saviour.

You cannot keep your mouth shut when you encounter God's love. The excuses we give for not sharing the good news are simply an indication that we don't know how loving our father is. When Zaccheus came in contact with this love he became a changed man. When the woman caught in adultery came in contact with this love she became transformed. When you come in contact with this love your life will never remain the same; sin will be unable to hold you down and you will reign over every trouble of life.

God has bridged the gap between you and him and he is waiting for you to receive his love. The same way Jesus had the woman in mind when he entered Samaria, when Jesus came to the Earth he had you in mind. Sin had separated you from him, but he didn't come to condemn you; he came to condemn sin so you will no longer be separated from him.

Do you have a track record of failing and falling? Well brace up yourself, it's time for your first success and the start of continuous victories. When you come in contact with Jesus the narrative will change. This woman who used to fail woefully when it came to men started succeeding with leading men to Christ, and isn't it amazing she didn't start with women?

God is saying to you 'the point at which you thought you failed I have chosen to use as a springboard for you. God is lifting you from your lowest point, and with you he is reaching others. Take a step of faith by resting on God's matchless, unconditional, irrevocable and eternal love for you, and you will see an avalanche of miracles pursue you on every side!

12

MY JESUS STORY

The best decision I ever made was to encounter the shepherd and lover of my soul. Life was empty, meaningless, and burdensome until I truly encountered him. As a young child, I grew up being nurtured and mentored by my Christian parents. They showed me what the Love of God meant, and early in my life, when I was ten(10) years old, I decided to follow and love the Lord Jesus Christ. I didn't fully understand what it entailed, I made it as a child and tried to uphold my decision with my strength, but I kept failing and stumbling. After I turned 20, I attended a conference where I finally understood the nitty gritty of my decision. I rededicated my life to the one who loves me beyond comprehension, Jesus Christ and it has been an adventurous journey ever since. Things might not have been perfect, but for me, Jesus Christ has been the best teacher, friend, and confidant anyone can ever have. He took fear away from my life and gave me so much peace. He gave me a reason for living and showed me that nothing is worth pursuing if he is not involved, nothing would be worth

trading my relationship with him for. I discovered that Christianity is not a religion but an experience and a relationship.
Chinedu MPA, USA.

I was born into a Christian family and grew up loving the Lord, yet I always felt there had to be more to the Christian life. Once a while, I would feel the arms of guilt and condemnation around me. I knew this wasn't what God wanted for me, but then I never knew how to go about experiencing freedom. I remember attending one of Pastor Signs' meetings. From where I was seated, I looked down at the altar as pastor screamed at the top of his voice, 'God is crazily in love with you!'. He invited us to make some confessions with him. That night, as I kept reciting those confessions with teary eyes, I was overwhelmed by the love of God. I knew that this was what I had been looking for. Since then, my life changed for good. I kept on listening to messages about how God loves me. I kept on seeking to know about what he did for me, and now I'm living a life free of guilt, shame. Now I'm full of the power of God. I have risen in the consciousness of what Christ has done for me, and my life has been beautiful.
Godsent, Nigeria.

As a Preacher's kid, I can hardly pinpoint an exact date of salvation, but I recall deciding to make things official at a children's camp meeting I had attended. Several years later when I encountered the truth of the Gospel, the Holy Spirit transformed my christian experience from mere religion to a true relationship. Following this encounter, prayers became understood, worship became fellowship, and fasting became joyous. My eyes opened to a new dawn of all the gloriousness in the Gospel of Christ, and how everything I need for life is contained inside this Gospel. My life has increased steadily, and this light shines effortlessly to all around me. Now, I know what it means to live a beautiful life regardless of happenings around you. Yet, knowing that I have not touched the tip of the iceberg of my glorious destiny makes me only wonder at how much God loves me.

Lisa, Israel.

I grew up in a Christian family, but this doesn't mean I have always walked in His power. Before I had a relationship with Jesus, I was depressed, self-loathing, self-harming, impure in speech and behaviour, and full of fear over many things. Jesus not only delivered me from depression, but healed me from deeply seated internal wounds by feeding my soul with His pure love and His words of life. Now, I am bold, courageous, walking in freedom and power, and cherish this body He has created for His glory. I am totally transformed and alive because of His mercy!

Grace, USA.

I remember praying the sinners' prayer as early as my primary school years. I kept having doubts however, about what it means to be saved and whether I was really saved. For a very long time, I was tormented by the fear of being left behind at Jesus' second coming. So every now and then I found myself rededicating my life to Jesus, or getting born again, again, just to convince my conscience that my salvation was still intact. In 2014, for the first time ever, I heard the gospel preached - the good news that all my sins were totally and completely forgiven! I encountered the Grace of God and He radically changed everything. Since then I have lived under the umbrella of God's perfect love and he has indeed cast out all fear.

Debby, United Kingdom.